Landlord Accelerated

How to create residual income that replaces your current salary in less than a year

Mary Bautista-Harman

ISBN: 978-1-928155-88-1

PUBLISHED BY:
10-10-10 PUBLISHING
MARKHAM, ON
CANADA

First Edition

Contents

Foreword	vii
Preface	ix
About Me	xi
Introduction	xv
Chapter 1: "You Are Here"	1
Chapter 2: "Job Security"	13
Chapter 3: Invest in YOU	23
Chapter 4: Your Mentor – Your Trusted Advisor	31
Chapter 5: Due Diligence – 360 degree views	37
Chapter 6: Power Team	49
Chapter 7: Market Value, Maths and Money	59
Chapter 8: Taking (the right) Action at the right TIME	73
Chapter 9: Putting It All Together	95
Chapter 10: Freedom: How I Did It	109
Summary	113
Testimonials	115
Reference Web Sites	117

Foreword

Few people would ever deny the importance of investing in property. In fact, you are unlikely to find anyone who has accumulated wealth without some type of investment in property.

There are several philosophies and strategies in the area of acquiring wealth through real property. Whatever vehicle you choose, you are in the driver's seat and you can take your life and your family's lifestyle wherever you want to go – if you plan ahead, arm yourself with the right people and resources, and get into action as quickly as possible.

We are fortunate to be living in a time when we can conduct business beyond borders, where we can learn locally and internationally, face to face, online and in books. The advent of technology allows us to speed up our education in our own time, often in our own living room.

And then it's time for ACTION.

Time is of the essence!

Speed is the secret ingredient of many successful ventures and transactions. "The early bird gets the worm" is an older adage, and truer today than ever.

In this book, investor Mary Bautista-Harman defies the odds by achieving a tremendous personal goal of financial freedom in a matter of ONE YEAR.

With "pedal to the metal" and laser-beam focus, Mary shows you how she managed to get educated, mentored and into action with break-neck speed AND cautious skepticism.

In addition to Mary's story, she provides insights and ideas to help you shorten your learning curve, save you from reinventing the wheel, and adopt a practical and consistent system that you can apply to your personal plan.

All you have to do is open the door and go, step by step.

This is the path taken by Mary Bautista-Harman. And it could be yours too!

...to your success!

Raymond Aaron
Author of Chicken Soup for the Soul, Real Estate Entrepreneur, National Speaker, New York Times Best Selling author.

Preface

I wrote this book for people who are very new to property investing and don't know what to do. I started late because I was afraid, uninformed, not connected and lacking confidence. But I did have desire. Lots of it! I wanted a passive income. I wanted to be self-sufficient. And I never realized that, even without my own money, I could start in the property business.

I've often heard that "You have to have money to make money." Perhaps money helps you stay afloat longer and bounce back more quickly, but it carries no weight against dedication, thoroughness, caution, research, patience, attention to detail and, above all, a burning desire to keep on keeping on.

About Me

This book is not an autobiography. It's actually about many people, possibly even you – and yes, about me too. It's about finding a way to get what you want… if you really want it.

Who am I? I'm an ordinary person: a daughter, a woman and a mother. I'm determined to have a good life, free of financial worry and free to spend more time with my family. Don't you want the same things for yourself and your family too?

My inspiration began in the Philippines where I was born. There I learned about sacrifice, generosity and love at a very early age. Out of necessity, to support our family, my mother moved to the UK, forwarding her nursing income to us back home.

Looking back, I see that my mother's courage and ambition were admirable. From where I sat as her daughter, though, I missed her, and I missed having a complete family and a stable home.

My passion for independence and closeness is what fuelled my inner fire going forward. I guess that's why I always wished I could settle in my own home.

***

I completed my education in the UK where I met my husband and started a family of my own. As an adult, with a husband, a son and a daughter, I was committed to find a way to stay close to them.

That meant finding a way to be an independent earner, working from home to generate a passive income I could rely on through the years.

The truth is that, even though I wanted this, I didn't really have the drive to get started until many years had passed. In fact, I was middle aged when I started.

When the recession struck, the local council for which I had worked for many years began to share various services with others to cut costs. Now I did not have a permanent position, only a two year contract by the end of which I would have to find another job, or…

I decided to move into property development, become self-employed and generate a passive income – all before my contract expired!

My short term goal was to have a passive income sufficient to live on by the time I reached the 'golden age' of 50. That way, I would be able to brag at my next high school reunion instead of feeling vaguely humiliated, while my classmates, who have become successful, high-flying lawyers, accountants and entrepreneurs boasted about their achievements!

And that's where my property story really began.

At this time I have several properties in the UK, the rent from which has replaced my previous salary – and I'm joint-venturing with my mother in the Philippines. We're building a 12-unit apartment for local people so we can help them.

I'm right on track!

My Purpose:

I was named after my aunt, a nun, Sister Mary Evelyn S.Sp.S. She is a missionary, like Mother Theresa, who helps the homeless and needy, and visits prisons. My father wanted me to follow her path.

Although I chose differently, she's been my inspiration, keeping me on the right path, always there to advise me spiritually, and to help me remain strong.

When I last went to the Philippines, I met my aunt and told her about this book; she was pleased. And I told her, "Auntie, this is my first book. I don't intend to make any money from it but if there are proceeds, I would like to donate them to your charity, to give something back."

I understand that to do that, I have to help myself first.

I hope this book will be an inspiration for people who are looking to get started in the property business. Don't wait. Start early, and start slowly, but do start.

For your journey, I'm hoping that I am among the "someones" you'll also learn from!

Introduction

Why have you picked up this book?

Was it the title that caught your eye?

Have you been wishing you could enjoy more quality time with your family and friends (knowing that wishing isn't enough)?

Have you dreamed of replacing your 9 to 5 job with passive income that will free you for other personal pursuits?

Or are you interested in investing in property, wondering how to start? Wondering if it's too late to start?

If so, you've chosen wisely.

Read on and I will share with you my personal experience of becoming a landlord and achieving a sufficient residual income in less than a year so I never need to work for anyone else again.

Chapter 1
"You are Here"

When I moved to England in 1989, I studied computing and got my degree. I was very keen to become employed straight away and earn money, so I accepted a post totally unrelated to what I had studied. I became a PA (Personal Assistant) for a firm of structural engineers and architects.

I did the usual administrative tasks, which included typing up building surveys and structural reports, encountering new, technical terms I had never come across before (and did not immediately understand), and clients who bought properties at auctions and refurbished them to rent or sell for profit.

I didn't really pay much attention to the business. I was just doing my job (that's J.O.B. – Just Over Broke) as a PA. I felt I could never do what these 'rich' property magnates were doing, as I didn't have their kind of money to get involved in real estate. I was just starting out in the 'j.o.b.' world, and I didn't intend to stay in this position. I had taken it only to gain experience and find an IT-related job eventually.

Little did I know I was planting the seeds for my independence! A year later, I tried to hand in my resignation, but every time I did so, my boss would give me a pay rise and I would stay. I must have been doing an exceptional job for the firm to give these pay rises for which I had never asked!

After five years in this same post, I promised my boss that I would find someone as good as I was, if he would let me go – so then he agreed.

Thereafter, I worked in the IT industry for over fifteen years in both the private and public sectors. Throughout, at the back of my mind, I had developed the desire to have a property portfolio of my own. I wanted to earn a passive income from property so I would have time to do what I really enjoy in life, working for myself, running my own business and having time to help other people.

When I married, my husband already had his own house, but I never really felt it was mine. So after putting a lot of effort convincing him to move, we chose to buy another house together that would be ours, mine as well as his, using our own money.

Then a few years later, when one of my husband's relatives passed away, he was involved in settling the estate.

All he could think of was selling the property.

All I could think of was how to buy and keep houses, including this one. It was really very affordable then. I should have, and could have, bought it. Now, with the benefit of hindsight, I see how many opportunities I never noticed before. And missed.

My mother-in-law sold her house very cheaply too. Since then, the value of her house has tripled – quadrupled, even.

For many years, I had wanted to invest in property, but I didn't know how. And so, I missed out on a number of opportunities. If I knew then what I know now, I'd already be prosperous… but I didn't and I'm not yet there – but I'm well on my way.

I had been in working in the IT industry for many years and have had numerous job titles, including programmer, IT consultant, principal infrastructure engineer, ICT school leader

– strategic and operation director and user systems administrator, among others. It was a great job and I managed the work, but I was not happy working for someone else.

Then, in November 2013, I attended a free two-hour property investment seminar.

Afterwards, I also participated in advanced courses to become even more educated in 'bricks and mortar' and in investing, whilst still working at my job in IT.

While some people take about a year to complete their education and mentoring, I was determined to move forward as quickly as possible, to do whatever it took to replace my income from my current job with a passive rental income.

That way, when I finished my IT work contract in June 2015, rather than worrying about finances and looking for a job working for someone else, I could have time to focus on my family, explore new business opportunities and become my own boss.

My property course ran from January 2014 until June 2014 and I successfully achieved my target within a year of starting my property business.

It was not all smooth sailing. There were – and are – many hurdles along the way. I'm writing this book so I can share my experiences with like-minded people, to inspire you to keep going, to focus and to remain positive. To build a productive and solid property portfolio, you will need a tremendous amount of commitment. When you make mistakes, build on them. Learn from them. Anyone can do it – even you! – if you invest in yourself, educate yourself in the business and have the right mindset.

Chapter 1

CREATING THE RIGHT MINDSET – Break the mould

If you're at all like me, you were taught to follow the leader. You did your schooling in order to get out there and make some money, and you imagined that all the pieces would systematically fall into place, as long as you did what others did before you: finish school, get a job for life, work until retirement age and collect your pension – the path of the historically traditional work/life cycle.

How much money do you want to earn? As much as possible? Or, more realistically, enough… enough to have a family, a lovely home, pay off the mortgage and any other debts, buy a luxury car, enjoy a four-week relaxing annual holiday, and then, at 65 (possibly later!): FREEDOM, retirement, a pension, choices, fun?

But will your pension pot be "full" enough for the lifestyle you want to have?

That was the dream!

Are you awake yet?

The media is telling us otherwise.

Reality bites. The "job for life" idea is a thing of the past, the "send in your resumé and you'll get an interview appointment, at least" was from another time, and the idea that life after retirement will be one long holiday, well, an idea whose time may never come.

I'm not speaking for everyone – just for everyone I've ever met!

Keep your eyes on the target and Focus on your Goal

When I took that first free property seminar, there were many "red lighters", naysayers, around me. But I was determined to learn how to earn a passive income and I couldn't think of other ways to do it.

I also found myself trying a number of network marketing businesses whilst doing my day job. I did make some money, but not enough to feel encouraged about reaching my goals.

MY GOAL:

I wanted never to have to worry about my monthly income again – and I set an ambitious goal: ONE YEAR! And I've done it!

My dedication and my results got the attention and interest of my husband, and already my daughter has decided that she wants to be an architect. My son is still deciding.

Where will your stairway take you? Why do YOU want to read this book?

My "WHY?"

If money were no object, what would you be doing in your life today?

If you removed FEAR from your mind, what would you do that aren't already doing?

In other words, why choose the uncharted, riskier, less predictable road? What is your WHY? If it's strong enough, you'll remain inspired, even if you have to brave snow and sleet to get to your goal.

A clear and strong "WHY" is a valuable personal motivating resource to strengthen your resolve in the face of overwhelm. It's about emotion and motivation, not logic.

On the other hand, if your WHY is wishy-washy, you'll be wishy-washy about working towards it – and is that trip really necessary?

'You can't hire someone to do push ups for you' – Jim Rhon

Property and its upkeep are major investments in time and in money. For some people, the idea of going through the hassles, the worries and the work makes the journey sound unpleasant – and unnecessary.

My WHY was big enough to pull me through that.

Are you feeling stuck and afraid in your work?

Are you frustrated with negative people guiding your career and making decisions that impact your life?

Tired of being the victim of someone else's schedule?

How excited are you about growing your own financial portfolio, your own business? How important is the freedom to create a new plan that meets your own hopes and dreams?

Why do you want this for yourself and your family?

Maybe you just don't want to live in an apartment anymore. Perhaps you have visions of your own house, your own garden.

What if you simply don't want to keep slaving away in the office until your time is up?

Get in touch with your own WHY.

Then the HOW will be an inspired pursuit.

My "HOW?"

HOW DO I GET STARTED?

It's human nature to be afraid of the unknown, to wonder if this is the right path to be on at any given time. It's part of personal development and growth.

Whenever there is something new to learn, we start out unaware. We don't know what we don't know. As we become familiar with the subject matter, we begin to see how much of the subject we don't know. Then with practice, research, exploration, commitment, discussion, experience, mentorship, application and successes – and some bruises here and there – we start to notice that we're actually starting to "get it", so we're aware that we're learning. And after extensive practice and application, bumps and successes, we become an "unconscious competent", someone who does the action, hits the opposition for six, completes a perfect round of golf, paints a mural, a "NATURAL".

Said differently, there are four basic stages of learning:

- **Unconscious Incompetent**
  We never thought about investing in real estate, so we didn't know what we didn't know, and we didn't care. We were unconsciously incompetent – on purpose.

- **Conscious Incompetent**
  When I started getting interested in investing, I was suddenly aware of the myriad of practices and disciplines that were involved in building, buying and selling property. Money, people, location, location, location, for starters...No wonder I was terrified. I was aware that I knew nothing!

- **Conscious Competent**
  After purchasing my first Buy to Let property I was fortunate to have a mentor to whom I could relate, and who was motivated to go through this with me. I was aware that I had learned so very much through this experience that I gained the confidence to do my next deals on my own.

- **Unconscious Competent**
  When Olympic skaters do their routine, they make things appear so easy, so smooth. It looks like it's effortless. Of course, it isn't, but it's so perfect, it looks so streamlined. For me, their warm-ups are awesome. Just floating around on the ice without a care or concern, and they aren't even aware they're gliding there.

For me, every move is an exercise in fear and focus, a way to fun, when I hope to relax and enjoy the skate.

In real estate, in some ways, every move is also an exercise in fear and focus on its way to fun. Although, never be lulled into the word "unconscious". Know what you know, and know what you don't know!

In other words, it takes diligent focus and action to become a "Natural" at something.

Where?
Where can I find the right information? Where should I invest?

There's so much information available these days – too much, even.

Where we used to have to look for information on real estate investing, today, information on real estate investing is looking for us – with offerings of courses, books, seminars, webinars and lectures, online, offline, in hard copy, e-books, even franchising! The challenge now becomes how to choose, whom to believe, where to begin.

Before venturing into your real estate business or investing in courses and books, do your research for FREE. Talk to people. Search the net. Listen to people. Attend networking events, presentations and sales promotion events. Ask questions. Get interested in other people's stories – the good and the bad, the successes, the failures and even the ones that got away!

Not only that, you never know whom you'll meet for business and personal, for clients, suppliers and partners. Everyone in those circles has a common interest: money! If you can create some synergies and more opportunities for learning and earning, it's all good!

I never knew there were such property networking events in UK until I was taking my advanced courses. I went to a few of these, including some in the neighbourhood where I invested. There are a couple that started in my local area and I was privileged to be invited to one – Property Investors Network (PIN) Sutton. I have now become part of the team of helpers who run it. And had I not been in touch with others, networking, connecting, I'd never have gotten the invitation – or even the information!

When?

The earlier the better. Waiting can cost you – in more ways than one.

Knowing and doing, though, are two different things. I would guess that most people try to set aside some of their hard-earned money for purposes down the road.

Have you already started building your personal retirement portfolio?

Are you already putting money into a savings account? And are you participating in any formal set-aside-for-a-rainy-day programs? Are you investing in tax-efficient savings like cash ISAs and stocks and shares ISAs? Maybe you've even been contributing to a company pension plan with visions of a worry-free retirement in ten, twenty or thirty years.

Do you have any idea if, how and when you'll be able to rely on it?

According to the changes we are already seeing in the wind, the financial future does not look rosy for people who rely on public and corporate pension schemes. Current legislation continues to infringe on the amount you can expect to earn, all the while calling for bigger contributions up front.

The Waiting Game can be expensive.

So WHY WAIT?

Many people begin with buying their first home. It's the easiest investment to acquire, calls for the smallest down payment, allows you to build up equity while replacing your rental payments with payments into your mortgage, and gives you a sense of confidence around managing, repairing, refinancing… Some people buy a home with the intention of renting it after a few years. They buy, live there for a while and move on to the next as part of their wealth strategy.

Generally speaking, these move-in-move-out strategies do not work for me. I'm not into frequent relocating. I've always wanted stability and my own home.

That's partly why I prefer not to do it that way.

If you don't plant today, nothing with grow tomorrow.

Chapter 2
Job "Security", golden handcuffs or ticket to ride?

"Your work is going to fill a large part of your life, and the only way to be truly satisfied is to do what you believe is great work. And the only way to do great work is to love what you do." – Steve Jobs

Do you love what you do?

The Hamster Wheel

I remember as a young person, listening and dancing to that catchy song "Working nine to five, what a way to make a living…." by Dolly Parton. Whenever it played on the radio, I perked up and danced to the beat, enjoying the music.

But I never really paid much attention to the words.

Now I do pay attention to the words and I don't work nine to five.

Every day, most people in the J.O.B. world have to follow a routine: get up early, prepare for work, rush into rush hour to make it on time to catch the bus or train, knowing that if you get a seat, it will be a miracle! Albeit a tiny one.

If you drive there, you must ensure you allow plenty of time to minimize the anxiety of sitting in endless traffic, or if you are lucky enough to live close to work, you run out at the last minute and fast-walk so you reach the office in time to get to your desk, turn on the computer, make a brew, greet your colleagues, get back to your desk, log in to the office system, check your email, check your calendar, check your voicemail… you have hardly started your day, yet it seems you are already exhausted from just reading the long 'to do list'.

If it's nine, you wish it were lunchtime; if it's five, you wish you were home. Monday, you wish for Friday; Sunday, you start to feel down, because the cycle starts again tomorrow morning… like the hamster running inside the wheel, always scurrying, getting nowhere.

If you are fulfilled in your job, if you're happy with your monthly salary and cost of living increases, if your benefits cover all your own and your family's expenses, if you're content with promotions every four or five years – and if you actually have a job that does that, year after year after year (and did I mention the "happy" part?) – Good for you! You have a positive path to follow, so keep following it. As long as you're happy and prosperous, confident that you're successfully taking care of your financial future, this book may not be for you.

On the other hand, if you don't relish the lengthy commute each way each day, if you wish you had more time and more energy – SOME energy – to enjoy your friends and family; if being overlooked for promotion has hurt you so many times you've stopped wanting to climb the corporate ladder where you work; or if you feel deflated because your ideas are set aside by people you don't respect, or even like, you may be ready to BREAK FREE. STOP! WAIT! And READ ON.

You, a link in a chain

Some people are clock watchers; they ensure their presence in the office precisely matches the exact minute of the working hours, not one second more than necessary. This may irritate you – the hard working ones – knowing that the clock watchers are on the same team, and on the same salary grade as you. You feel that you work longer hours than they do, you complete more daily tasks than they do, but still get the same remuneration at the end of the month – sound familiar? It sucks, doesn't it? But you have to follow the flow, rather like the soldiers in a regiment, just working along, following your employer's rules, thinking you need this JOB to pay the bills, so you just do your bit, do the best you can, and hope that your bosses will notice how productive you are compared to the others, so they'll award you a pay rise.

If you work for the private sector, you may be given incentives or bonuses for your hard work. If you work for local government, however, the chances are that, no matter how hard you work, or the long hours you put in to complete your projects on time, you will not get a bonus or a pay rise – there is no such thing, unless you apply for a vacant job post that pays more than your current scale.

Your Employer, pulling your chain

Your employer may think you're fortunate to even have a job; to be devoting all your time and energy to earn that salary.

In fact, the opposite is quite true. We are working to earn enough money to cover us until the next pay day, taking one baby step at a time, placing one foot in front of the other, trading your irreplaceable hours for pounds, dollars, euros, pesos, yen, or whatever currency you use.

When you realize that you're following a road leading nowhere, you may feel stuck, resentful, disappointed – and worse; scared, resigned, hopeless.

Instead, take a serious look at WHY you're still working for "the boss".

You can turn these negative feelings into positives. In fact, you must!

And the truth is, there are some great reasons to stay in your job a while longer. Some people call it "security".

Your job may not fulfil your dreams at this time. But before jumping ship, think about your job as a ticket to ride... a ticket to FREEDOM. Think of your job as a VOYAGE, not a destination.

And, as a VOYAGE, your job can help take you where you want to go. But without the vessel you could be stuck in the harbour. So please reread the previous paragraph, take a deep breath, and enjoy the voyage!

Get started whilst you have a job.

Some people get so excited about the potential of investing in real estate that they want to quit their job immediately and start buying property, so they can start raking in the cash. (Don't we all?)

Like any other venture, though, there are a few ways to get there, some of which are more responsible than others. Quitting and diving in is not one of the more responsible ones.

Having a traditional j.o.b. is a great way to become established, build credit, accumulate cash, and gain some property experience, with the security of that regular salary. In other words, until you're steadier on your feet, start small, start manageably – but START.

Following rules? OR Building on them?

You may have heard the phrase "If it ain't broke, don't fix it." There's another variation: If it ain't broke, BREAK it!

In other words, if everything in your job world is going fine, great; as long as it works for you.

BUT

If your job pays the bills but doesn't do anything for you on any other level, feel free to break the mould and break free!

When you classify your employment as a step towards greatness, you can be happier following the rules while always looking ahead for ways to capitalize on what's there.

Do you get a regular lunch break at work? What if that became a regular "networking break" or a "market research" or "study" break?

Do you leave work at 5 pm? Stop by the library on your way home.

Do you start your day at 9 am? Start at 8 and squeeze in some mentoring time.

In other words, while you are still on the job and following the rules, CREATE YOUR OWN!

Timing is everything, so start early – especially while you are on someone else's payroll.

HOW LONG WILL YOU STAY THERE?

The earlier you start in the "property game", the more time you have to compound your investments, to take more risks (and recover from a failure or two), to build your portfolio, and to get rich.

Remember the words of Napoleon Bonaparte "I may lose a battle, but I shall never lose a minute."

You need to make a strong commitment so you can withstand the bumps along the road. And there will be bumps.

How long will you remain on the sidelines before jumping in with two feet? How much time will you devote to preparing, learning, seeking, networking, before taking action?

While you're still on the job, you can prepare yourself with education and insights as a foundation. Learn the essentials so you can get started quickly. How long will that take? Set a goal of a few months, maximum one year.

Choose a date for transitioning from your existing job to your investing job. Commit to this timeline. In fact, tell your family and friends that you are planning to be out of this and into that by the end of one year. This disclosure creates clarity, can hold you accountable, and also prepare your circle of contacts to be aware of trends, opportunities, or deals that you might be interested in.

PLAN YOUR WORK – PLAN TO LEAVE YOUR WORK!

My plan was and is to replace my job income with property rental income, so my initial niche is to buy and let houses for passive income.

My plan attempts to answer each of the following key questions:

1. What is the strategy and the model for my property investment business?
2. How will I raise extra capital for more acquisitions?
3. What is a good deal? What objective deal criteria will I stick to?
4. Who are my target tenants? What do they really want? Where are they looking to live?
5. How will I find prospective deals? How will I find the best tenants?

When I don't have good answers, I go back to my mentors, my local professionals and my education resources to help me find them.

There's no such thing as the "one perfect deal". Real estate is everywhere. The one commodity you cannot replace is TIME. Time for your property to appreciate. Time for your money to compound. Time to make mistakes and recover from them. Time to multiply your experiences to generate enough cash flow to sustain and build on.

You could start sooner than you think

If you're young and looking to purchase a new home to live in, maybe you should consider why your first home should be an investment property instead. Most people wait until after they've bought their first or second home to begin investing in real estate. You can start much sooner than you think.

Find out how much you can afford

That way, you can leverage where you are now, with a poor credit rating, a depressingly modest lifestyle and limited responsibilities, into an actual investment giving you lots of flexibility and time to manage your responsibilities more effectively.

YOU HAVE TO LIVE SOMEWHERE

The money you're now spending "living the life" in a rented apartment could be spent on "building the life". At this stage, your lifestyle allows for saving and planning that might be impossible later because you'll have more obligations then.

What if you started with your own home?

You're already paying rent month in and month out. If you do the maths and calculate the return – zero! – you'll start to get the notion of getting into the game early.

For many people, buying their first home is part of a traditional progression through adult life. The idea of leveraging a first home as an investment goes against some people's general view of the future:

- Complete formal education
- Job
- First rental, Second rental, Third rental
- Marriage
- Starter Home (or fourth rental)

- Children
- Second Home
- Children's Education
- Investments (if you can afford them)
- Retire

This journey gives you lots of time to do your thing while you're young, even making decisions you might not make if you'd "known then what you know now".

But if you compare waiting to start putting your income to work for you against how much your investment property could increase in value while also supplying you with rental income, you'll start to get the picture of "why wait?" What are you waiting for?

You can lay the foundations solidly, carefully, mindfully, and build a stairway step by step, investing intelligently in assets that appreciate year after year while your job qualifies you for the leverage you'll need to really make this happen.

Your job does give you some choices while you're learning to "fly solo". You have some money coming in, which you can rely on for the moment. That's almost peace of mind.

Turn that semi-peace-of-mind into a stepladder taking you up to the launch pad for your own investments: in yourself, in your family, and in your financial wellbeing through property.

Your creditworthiness looks much better when you're employed and earning. You can qualify for larger mortgages, your position as a joint venture partner has more credibility, and you might be able to attract more investment opportunities because your income is verifiable on paper.

So it's a great idea to phase out regular employment gradually, all the while reinforcing your resolve with reading and research to increase your readiness to "jump ship".

DON'T SAY GOODBYE FOREVER

When you do finally leave your regular day job, you have the added advantage of connecting with your former colleagues to help them leverage their own salaries into sustainable passive income from property investment.

Celebrate your j.o.b. so you can become free.

… and don't forget to switch off the light on your way out. Hurrah!

Chapter 3

Invest in YOU

TIME = MONEY
Until you have money, leverage your time.

Successful people know that investing in themselves is one of the best investments they can make. Next is investing in property.

HOW MUCH ARE YOU PREPARED TO INVEST IN YOURSELF?

Training gurus have been stating that it takes 10,000 hours to learn any new skill to proficiency.

If you study investment as a full-time student, at a thirty-hour week, you'll be up to your eyeballs in studying for about six years!

In addition, how much time can you set aside for a job to keep you going?

To become investment-savvy, can you devote thirty hours per week to study AND maintain your full-time job? OR can you afford to forfeit your job income and jump into your studies? (If you can, perhaps this book isn't for you.) Being realistic, adding more stress to your day, and to your job (including that lengthy hour commute daily), maybe you could devote just one hour each night (if that much). That's 365 hours a year, or TWENTY SEVEN years before you get to 10,000 hours.

So you need LEVERAGE. And where do you get leverage to save time? From other people's time, and learning what they learned from that time so you don't have to start from scratch.

CASE STUDY:

I was shy. I've never liked standing in front of many people – and I wanted to conquer that fear. There's a Toastmasters club where I used to work. I didn't have to pay money to participate; I simply invested my time. Although I was busy with my job and my family, I made time to join, and attended as many meetings as I could. That's where I faced and overcame my fear, and developed my skills in speaking in front of an audience. Now I'm much more confident, as long as I have a prepared speech. As elsewhere, preparation is key.

There are no guarantees that knowledge of property ins and outs will make you rich. But in this business, "ignorance is NOT bliss".

Without proper education in property investing, you could be easily making significant mistakes that could damage your wallet and your self-confidence.

Find a mentor. Although it might not be obvious to you at this early stage, having a mentor is a major part of investing in yourself. More about mentors in the Power Team chapter.

Here's how I took my first steps:

It was a free 2-hour property seminar that planted the seed and got me thinking about opportunities in property investment for me, and for my family's wellbeing.

I became an avid knowledge seeker, researching information online, watching webinars on YouTube.

Then I decided that it was the right time to learn the business, so I attended the advanced property courses, which also included mentoring.

It cost a lot! I nearly fell off my chair as I handed over my credit card. Then it occurred to me that both my children had gone to private school and we had paid for their education, so why not do the same for myself and my own education and learning?

And when I asked if I could get my money back, she nodded and said, "Yes... if you follow what's being taught." I was trembling. I couldn't sleep that night, to be honest. She was that confident that I would be able to recover my investment – which I have. It was a huge investment which I kept secret, not even telling my husband until after I had been successful in a deal or two.

The system works!

Here's an overview of my path:

- Saw paper advertisement for free property seminar.
- Took advanced Property Education courses. I found mine in the local newspaper: the founder is a successful woman with a vision that resonated with me, to help people. I liked her values and ethics, and my selection turned out to be the right one.
- Found a mentor, followed their advice, took them to inspect and troubleshoot properties, and then redid calculations a few times; to make sure the maths were correct.
- Studied the big picture and local demographics of my target market.

- Researched how much local development and regeneration were being planned or were already in progress; investigated availability of local employment and population growth.
- Mapped my market; highlighted best locations.
- Asked letting agents about the most desirable areas that tenants wanted (Chapter 5).
- Reviewed their process for valuing a house. I learned this in the property course and it was interesting to compare from a different perspective.
- Asked questions, especially about the biggest mistakes to avoid.
- Do your desktop research of as many as 50 properties and then visit them in person, once you've done your comparables and identified which are most interesting for your objectives.

When you're sure you have a positive cash flow property that suits your personality and portfolio profile, do the maths, get the facts, and DIVE IN!

What investment are you prepared to make, in time and in money, to create the right foundation on which you'll build your "empire"?

There are organizations of people with similar interests and needs where you can get information and help. You will want to join these groups for your own education, for networking and to establish your credibility. This is where you will meet people for joint ventures, for contacts, and even to find tenants.

Become accredited with organisations such as National Landlord Association (NLA), Landlord Accreditation Wales (LAW) – this will soon be rebranded as 'Rent Smart Wales' –

Decent and Safe Housing (DASH in Nottingham), or any other recognised associations as well as networking groups in your area for local insights and connections. Note that you will normally have to attend a course, or a representative from the organisation (e.g. DASH) will visit your property to ensure it is safe to live in and compliant with current housing regulations, and/or undergo certain written or online examinations and pass them before you get awarded with accreditation status.

Other learning resources abound.

Become a voracious reader and researcher to keep on getting the best of the best: study property books, journals, newspaper and magazine articles. Join property related groups on social media like Facebook, Linked In and elsewhere. You can also learn a surprising amount from watching property-themed television programmes such as 'Homes Under the Hammer', 'Location, Location, Location', 'Grand Designs' and 'Selling Houses'; and obtain information such as the warning signs of subsidence and/or damp that will need to be rectified as a matter of urgency and will increase your renovation budget considerably, learn which areas tend to have cheaper properties and gain inspiration by seeing how others have renovated and improved their properties. For me, watching these programmes also improved my very limited knowledge of the geography of the United Kingdom, introducing me to places I had never heard of and knew nothing about, which I have since visited – and where I now own rental properties!

One of the amazing aspects of property investing is that anyone can do it. You don't need a degree, you don't need a licence, you don't even need to use your own money!

But you do need the right mindset, determination, hustle, stamina, contacts, guts, deals, and "smarts".

Some people seem to be "naturals" when it comes to vetting investment numbers and possibilities. I think of those as "street smarts". Things they learned by doing, connecting, watching, asking.

Then there's more formal smarts; lessons to help you understand how to analyze a property, process the maths, assess reports, present options, compare proposals and sale documents.

The combination of Formal Smarts and Street Smarts gives you the 360 degree vision you need to apply as you build your property portfolio.

If successful investing is your vision, your goals need to also be SMART.

Specific, Measurable, Achievable, Realistic, and Timely.

By documenting your ideas, your dreams, your plans and clearly detailing their SMART details, you'll be better prepared to remain on course to your chosen destination.

Without a clear path, any direction will do... and that is an unacceptable idea that simply will not do!

SPECIFIC:
I was very clear that I wanted to invest in property without using my own home as security for a mortgage and to generate a passive income from property that would replace my salary from regular employment.

MEASURABLE:
I knew that my employment income was £x, so my target profit had to be £x

ACHIEVABLE:
I had only been working part-time, so my annual income was not impossible to replicate using this strategy. Without the reading, researching, courses – and my mentor, of course – I might have allowed myself to deny that this was achievable. I was fortunate to have surrounded myself with achievers!

REALISTIC:
If I had young children at the time, or if we had had to take on debt to purchase our own home, "R" might have been a sticking point in my goal setting. As it happens, this was all very realistic. I've proven that.

TIMELY:
There is no time like the present, to learn, to earn, to explore, to network, to commit and to get results. I was only working part-time, so I was able to devote time to property investing courses and commencing my strategy before leaving employment.

And I do have the results I targeted so far.

And yes, I sometimes do feel SMART.

Chapter 4
Your Mentor – Your Trusted Advisor

The best way to avoid making mistakes is to learn from those who already made mistakes of their own.

"Fools say they profit from their mistakes, I have always made it my business to profit from the mistakes of others," German Chancellor Otto von Bismark once said.

Learn from other people. That's how I got started. That's how I got over the fear. That's how I made fewer mistakes. (Although I still made some of my own – and so will you…)

Your mentor is someone who can take you by the hand and point the way for you, for your own situation, for your particular goals. Your mentor listens to you and is there to help you get to where you want to be.

They know they can, because they've been there – in your shoes. Some advisors and sales people disguise themselves as mentors. They provide information and ideas, but they don't necessarily have your interests at heart, so choose yours wisely, verify references on and offline, and know that not all mentors are created equal.

CASE STUDY:

When I attended my advanced property course I was informed that I would be assigned a mentor. I specified that I wanted somebody in a similar situation to myself. I was alone in this property journey, as my husband didn't want to get involved because he didn't want to have another mortgage. I needed someone to hold my hand and guide me through. I was told that there was only one person in the team of mentors who could match my requirements, so she was assigned to me.

We had emails and Skype communications initially, followed by a two-day intensive meeting that concentrated all the interactions deeply and quickly. For me, that was sufficient.

I was not interested in monthly updates or long-term coaching. I wanted to fast track – and also, I didn't want to have to pay for extra mentor time.

GETTING ADVICE:

Look for advice from property experts before you invest. They will have insights into the local marketplace, often with information and examples of the types of property that are more likely to appreciate in value.

Successful people often enjoy sharing and mentoring. They are excited, happy, proud of their accomplishments – and they love to tell stories. Look for opportunities to connect with them, at a special event or a book signing perhaps.

Volunteer to be a helper at upcoming seminars and events in your local area. Connect with them on LinkedIn and Facebook. Ask thought-provoking questions and provide positive and appreciative comments. Become familiar to them if you can.

Higher profile investors often host networking events as introductions to programs, seminars, services and sometimes properties they want to sell. Go to these events and find out what's happening behind the scenes. Listen to the questions being asked. In fact, make it a point to meet these people. They could be valuable team members as you create your power team.

You can find out through networking, attending property investment network meetings, meeting them at courses and special events, mentoring groups, among others.

Some investors write books, host webinars, or have websites that offer newsletters.

Network with like-minded people to raise your profile and meet more potential partners and investors at local property meetup groups, at property seminars and courses and at other property-specific events. You can find these advertised in your local newspaper, online, and even simply by asking people you know who are associated with the industry.

Copy what these experienced successful people are already doing to avoid the pitfalls they experienced along the way. That way you can accelerate your property investing success without making the mistakes of people who went before you.

Remember, though, that you are in the driver's seat. You are the person "on the line". Network, learn, then choose wisely.

Always confirm, monitor, and keep records of every step along the way. You can follow someone else's path and try their ideas, but each situation is unique and deserves its own focus and attention. One thing you don't want is a surprise. More often than not, surprises hurt!

CASE STUDY

At the beginning, whenever I viewed a house, I would become overwhelmed by the things needing fixing, even the smallest details. But on days I spent with my mentor, I could position the work differently to keep things simple.

My mentor saved me from going too far off track, although I was in the driver's seat throughout.

The house that I was initially going to buy was a six-bedroom townhouse fitted out as an HMO for students. It had originally been bought to provide accommodation for the owner's children while they were at university. It was already tenanted but all the students were leaving at the end of that academic year, so the owners were selling.

On paper, the return and cash flow looked great – positive.

But the nature of the property limited its appeal. It was bugging me for a while.

Here's what I learned:

This particular property was a leasehold with a covenant that stated that it could only be let to students. So if there was a shortage of students and I had vacancies, I would not be permitted to let to a family or professionals, only students.

Also, as a leasehold, there were numerous other restrictive covenants, for example: *'not to hold any political religious charitable or other meeting on the Premises or to use the Premises for dancing music or singing lessons or practice providing that this clause shall not prohibit prayer meetings twice daily over a period of seven days following the funeral of either of the tenants'!*

I actually met the student landlords and their mother who managed the property. They were very nice people. I told them I wanted their property and they were very happy, ready to sell right away. They were desperate to sell, and I was getting emotional about the intensity of the connection.

Fortunately my mentor came with me and together we examined the place.

When I found out about the leasehold problem and its restrictions, I had to back out. I did not want to be stuck with vacancies I could not fill. And since occupancy was restricted to students, if I didn't fill the place at the beginning of the academic year, I would have to carry a void period for the rest of the year, and that was not part of my master plan.

Even so, I was pulled in the direction of the property.

My mentor had to remind me that this is a business, that emotions had no place in this negotiation, and that the limitations would limit my flexibility. So I chose to pull out.

The emails that followed between the vendor and me were volatile, about wasting time and money. The words were angry, super-charged with emotion and sounded offensive, to the point where I actually was reconsidering the purchase.

My mentor helped me remain strong and aloof. This was a business decision. In spite of having paid for services to assess the property, my mentor suggested that I simply cut my losses and move on. Nothing personal, just business.

Chapter 5
Due Diligence – 360 Degree Views

Many people think of due diligence as it relates to money. Actually it's about researching, confirming, comparing, validating.

That said, the road is fraught with hurdles and grey areas.

- Take nothing for granted. Even if it's in writing. Especially if it's in writing.
- Research the area – schools, transport links, hospitals, people, crime, development plans
- Assess "great" deals with real comparisons, historical details, amenities, rentability

TENANT DUE DILIGENCE:

One of the more important aspects of getting the right property to let is determining tenant demand in the area. Look for a town or city where demand is greater than supply. Check the latest local inspection reports and talk to local people. Are you near transport links, good schools, for example?

NEIGHBORHOOD DUE DILIGENCE:

If you want to let to a family, what's the labour market like in the area? Are you near universities if your target market is students? And near shops, town or city centre, transport links, hospitals etc., for working and professional tenants? That way, you can almost guarantee that prospective tenants will find you at the same time as you are trying to find them.

If you think that you don't have time to do location research and other due diligence, MAKE time to do this! You'll be surprised that even just ten minutes here and there can make an important difference. If you work full-time, get someone to work on your behalf. If you work part-time, you have no excuse and can spend more time on this crucial area.

Here are some ways to research location:

Online – visit property websites online. You don't need to physically visit locations on your initial research. You can source properties from your desk during your work break or even during commercial breaks when watching television at home. If you have a tablet computer, you might be able to multi-task with other activities (women seem to be better able to do this, to an extent – sorry men!). These sites usually provide a lot of information, including pictures of the house, the location, the type of people who live there, people and area statistics and demographics, sold and rent houses comparables. Examples of these sites are: Rightmove and Zoopla.

Estate Agents – talk to estate agents in your chosen area. They are most willing to help you with your search if they understand that you are a serious prospective buyer. If they have no available houses currently, make sure you are on their mailing list so they can send you notification alerts as soon as a suitable one becomes available. Getting early information from estate agents is also an opportunity to acquire property below the market value. For example, if they have a property that has been in the market for a very long time, they could be representing a more motivated seller, which means a better price for you. Make sure you find out why the house is not selling: Are the sellers actually motivated? Are they desperate to sell their house quickly? Some of these houses may have just come in and have not yet been advertised nationally.

Letting Agents – Your best source of information for location and to find your desired type of tenants who can afford the rent level you wish to obtain are the letting agents. Some Estate Agents have a separate letting agent department. I would personally approach letting agents separately from Estate Agents, and enquire if they have a waiting list of tenants looking for houses in a particular location. Once information is provided, you can zero in on it and then research that particular area. Armed with more information, you can then approach Estate Agents about any houses they may have available for sale.

Talk to Local People. If you live in an area where you intend to invest, you may already know the most desirable locations, the house prices, tenant demographics and demands and lifestyle. They will soon tell you which areas have a bad reputation, whereas an estate agent trying to sell properties there will not! This is how I avoided buying a property in a certain part of Nottingham.

But if your chosen location is further away and you are unfamiliar with the area, the best method to find information is to attend any of your local property networks or property meetings. You are more likely to connect with other investors who might have properties in that area, and who can give you advice on the desirable and not so desirable areas for investment. Not only that, these landlords may have already connected with reliable teams of tradesmen, such as local builders, plumbers, electricians, handymen; and also with letting agents, estate agents, mortgage brokers and solicitors. Talk to as many people as you can.

Case Study: VIEW, VERIFY AND VALIDATE

My first BTL was about 3 hours from my home. That distance generated a concern about finding tenants who would care for my place as if it were their own, who would look after the property with pride, and who I could get to on short notice should the need arise.

So prior to closing the deal, I made it a point to stay near the property for a few days, to give me a better feel about the area as if I were living there myself.

That way I got a clearer sense of who my tenants were, the type of person in the neighbourhood, and the ins and outs of the area where the property was located. These insights were very helpful as I worked with local tradespeople and my local tenants, with greater understanding and affinity.

PROPERTY DUE DILIGENCE

Before you decide to buy a property, you should be aware of a range of issues that could impact your decision.

For example, in Wales, there is an outbreak of an invasive plant called Japanese Knotweed. It is an extremely prolific and strong plant that can grow astonishingly quickly and can push through concrete and damage buildings, roads and pavements.

In fact this has become so much of a problem that many mortgage lenders are now refusing to mortgage a property where the weed is present, or even one where it is nearby. If Japanese Knotweed is located within 6 metres of the house, the value of the property is severely reduced and nobody will buy it.

The infestation can only be controlled by ongoing spending to attempt to clear it up, which is both expensive and difficult, because if one small part of a root is left behind a new plant will grow and prosper. So Japanese Knotweed is a definitely a deal-breaker.

Case Study

Last year I was going to buy the student house next door. In fact, I even put in an offer, which was rejected. Several months later, it was still on the market, so I was able to submit an offer well below market value. This offer was accepted. Then I learned that the property had Japanese Knotweed.

We decided to have a complete survey done to assess the damage. There was a lot of the weed growing at the back of the property – and all the way up a hill to the back.

I contacted the Welsh Council about the knotweed invasion, to see if they could do anything and provide a program to deter ongoing growth. I was advised and reassured in writing that they would tackle the issue in the Spring and every year thereafter.

Japanese Knotweed grows so quickly that when we visited the area in the early summer, I discovered that not all of the weeds had been killed and there was more work to be done.

In the end, I chose to pull out of the deal next door because the treatment had not done its work to kill the weed, and because the builder's assessment of the work that needed doing in the house was that it would be extremely costly.

I still did (and do) own the other house in the area; fortunately, there is no knotweed on my side.

Even then, I was advised by the letting agent not to buy more in the area because the university was going to relocate. The information sounded credible, but I wanted to confirm this information.

I actually contacted the university to validate the information. Most prospective investors would not take this extra step. However, until you have the information from the source, it's all just rumours.

Soon after I pulled out of the deal, I met the new landlord who had purchased the property. He seemed to know what he was doing and, since he already lives in Wales, we exchanged contact information and continued to communicate.

He told me that the new university was being built farther away, but that it would be in addition to the existing one.

With his first-hand insights and knowledge, he started to refurbish the property with a new kitchen, a new roof and total renovation in order to prepare a higher standard property for a higher standard tenant.

As a result, where students were previously moving away, now that row of houses is becoming more appealing, and more marketable.

It turned out that the campus closing rumour was just that – a rumour. I was very relieved, of course, and now I am optimistic about locating great tenants in the area for my great property.

Never accept details on surface information. It's worth the investment to dig deeper, even if you have to walk away. Negotiate when you find something below your expectations.

Love at first site? What to look for when viewing a house

1. **Take plenty of photographs**: If you are viewing several properties in one day, take a photo of each house: the front of the house with the number if available clearly visible, the roof from ground level, the rooms, all the obvious defects you can see and the back of the house, so that when you come to review them afterwards, you'll remember which one is which. Viewing several houses can become confusing!

2. **Check the roof:** Replacing roofs is expensive, and newer roofs have a life expectancy of only 15-20 years, depending on the materials. Ask how old is the house. Does it have the original roof? How old is the roof? Are there any tiles or slates missing? Check the ridgeline along the top of a pitched roof: if it's not straight, but sags in the middle, the roof timbers may not be strong enough to support the weight of the tiles and may need to be replaced or strengthened. If the property has a flat or nearly flat roof, check out the material with which it is sealed and find out when it was last recovered. Nowadays a membrane is used and is better than asphalt and gravel, which can leave seams and edges unsealed. If you own a drone with an on-board camera, you could obtain a far better view of the roof than a surveyor could achieve!

3. **Check for dampness:** As you enter the property, are there any of the following signs of damp: a musty mouldy smell, flaky plaster, watermarked walls or ceilings?

It sounds obvious, but make sure you look closely at and around the ceiling and around the skirting boards. Brown damp stains on a ground floor ceiling suggest there has been a leak – probably from a bathroom or central heating pipe in the past.

Ask whether it has been fixed. Such stains on an upstairs ceiling should alert you to problems with the roof or guttering. Damp in ground floor walls usually indicates the failure of the damp proof course or – in older properties – the absence of one.

This can be rectified by injecting the walls to create a new damp proof course, but will require the removal of internal plaster to a height of one metre before injection, replastering and redecoration afterwards, so you will need to allow for the additional expense of longer refurbishment time. Have any rooms been repainted, possibly to conceal damp? I have invested in a damp meter and normally take this with me when doing my property viewings, to prod walls with suspected damp.

4. Does the building look structurally sound? If the house looks and feels solid and structurally sound, and has no large cracks on the walls, you may not need to obtain a full structural survey. You should expect some hairline cracks on internal plaster, particularly in older houses. Look especially around where extensions join onto the original walls, end-of-terrace walls, and bay windows, all of which can start to fall or bow away from the rest of the house. If you see major cracks, the walls look like they are seriously bowing or you have any doubts, it might be worth engaging a structural engineer to check the house.

5. Can you flush the toilet? How long does it take for the water to come through? Does the toilet flush work?

6. Is the plumbing up to scratch? Run the taps to check the water pressure. Ask if the pipes are insulated, and ensure they are not lead (which would have to be replaced). Do the radiators actually work? How old is the boiler? If the hot water tank is situated in the roof it is probably an old one, and may have to be replaced soon.

7. **Is there sufficient natural light in the house?** Which way does the house face? In winter, during a cloudy day or at night, it is difficult to tell the difference between a north and south facing house or garden – but in summer it can make the difference between a home that is full of light and warmth, and one that is dark. Take a compass, or your phone may have already have an app; if not, get one.

8. **How big are the rooms?** If the house is occupied, some vendors put smaller furniture into rooms to make them seem bigger. Bring a measuring tape and measure the room if you can. If a room is sufficiently large, could you partition it with a stud wall to create another room to add value to the house?

9. **Do the window frames have cracking paint?** Is the double-glazing intact? The state of the external window frames is a great indicator of the state of the house – if people look after those, they are likely to have taken great care of the rest. If you can easily push your finger into wooden window frames, they are usually rotten. If there is condensation between double-glazed window-panes it means that they are faulty.

10. **Check the condition of the wiring:** Dodgy wiring can be dangerous, and rewiring your new home can be an expensive business. Check out the fuse board; does it look old and outdated?

11. **Is there a loft?** People often ignore the loft or attic, but it is an important part of the house. How easy is it to access? Is there much storage space? Could it be converted into extra rooms? Is there sufficient insulation?

12. **What's the area like?** Are you near a **pub** or **bar** or **kebab** shop that becomes rowdy in the evening?

Can you walk to shops to get a pint of milk, or do you have to drive?

Is it easy to get to public transport?

Are there noisy roads or train tracks nearby?

Are you underneath a flight path?

And most importantly, does it feel like you or your tenants could live there?

If you do like a property, arrange another viewing for a different time of day, and check out the locals. If you can, take a builder or surveyor with you who might be able to notice things you don't and who can assess how much work it needs.

FINANCIAL DUE DILIGENCE

Understand your property's financial status. Look beneath the surface and source your own numbers.

Have you ever been presented with a great-looking cash flowing property only to find out later that it's actually not all that it seems?

Check out the financial breakdown in Chapter 7 for a real example of a deal I actually considered – until I did the maths. Another important thing to remember in buying an income-generating property is to understand its financial status. Quite often, we are presented with a standard 'template' of financial information, demonstrating examples of purchase cost, cash flow, and return on investment. These are only illustrations of how the property 'may' perform. Smart investors only buy properties based on the 'actual' performance.

CASE STUDY

In one particular almost-sold example, the estate agent could not (or would not) provide the responses to my questions: Why is the owner selling, when it's already tenanted and generating income?

I then visited the property and brought a builder with me. I found that the place was not well kept, that the rooms looked pretty pokey, the bathroom filthy, damp stains on the ceiling, and a lot of work that needed doing throughout the property.

There happened to be a letting agent board displayed at the front of the house, so I took the opportunity to enquire about the current tenants, how much monthly rent they were paying per room and whether they pay their own utility and other bills above or inclusive of the rent.

The letting agent was extremely helpful and informative. I was able to find out that the landlord pays for all the bills (gas, water, electrics, council tax). After having done my sums, the net return on investment was almost falling into negative. Not only that, the current occupants were not exactly my ideal tenants, according to the profile I had created for my desired candidates.

Needless to say I chose not to proceed with this particular purchase, saving my investment for something more closely aligned with my preferences. That way I saved myself taking on someone else's problems!

CASE STUDY

I first found an HMO that was already occupied by students, so it showed an existing cash flow. I was interested, naturally, and put in an offer which was accepted.

But when I had the full structural report completed, I realized there was a lot to repair. I renegotiated and achieved a discount from the asking price, about £10K below market value. I was able to generate over 15% net return from my first "HMO Cash Machine".

So it's really critical to do your due diligence, not just the area but the financial aspect.

Chapter 6
Power Team (It takes a Village...seems like...)

Efficient management of your property is crucial to your peace of mind – and to your wallet!

As a property owner, you could save some money by being your own property manager. It's a great way to learn at first (I did that!), but in the longer term, is that really what you want for yourself?

Managing your own rental property has its challenges, 24/7. Do you really want to spend your time being hands-on, with all its ins and outs and ups and downs?

The good news is: you don't have to do it alone – or even at all. You can employ a managing agent who can do the full letting management for you so you can be free to do what you are good at.

You can't do everything on your own, so hire people who are expert at things that you are not good at. It's essential to have a property power team around you that you can trust and upon whom you can rely, to ensure your properties and tenants are being well looked after. Your power team consists of professionals that you use for the day-to-day running of your business. Here are some of the key individuals that you should have in your power team:-

ESTATE AGENTS – how you can get them on your side

Estate agents work for the sellers but they only earn their commission when they succeed in selling a property to a buyer. If you can get an estate on your side as an investor, it can help you be first in the queue when viewing houses – and can also help you negotiate a better price.

1. **Arrange to meet with the agent.** It's important to know the local estate agents in the area where you want to purchase. Visit their office, sit down and discuss your requirements face-to-face. That way, when you telephone them, the more likely they are to remember you. For the most part, people prefer to deal with people they already know. So be known.

2. **Demonstrate that you are a serious buyer from the start.** Show that you are a keen, serious buyer and not a time waster. Estate agents expect you to have proof of funds or have arranged your mortgage in advance, even before making an offer on a property. This tells estate agents that you can act quickly, and puts you right at the front of the estate agent's mind when new properties come onto the market.

3. **Swap contact details.** Make sure you obtain the individual agent's name, mobile phone number and email. This will not only ensure you always have a point of contact, but will also allow you to develop a relationship with them. It is easier to deal with an individual than the whole staff of an office. Give them your contact details and an idea of the sum of money you are prepared to spend. (You don't have to disclose the full details of your financial situation as this could actually put you at a disadvantage in negotiations if they know you can afford more.)

4. Give them your requirements. In the first contact tell them what type of property you are looking for, and which area(s) you would most like to invest in. Make clear on which requirements you will not compromise, and which you are prepared to be flexible about.

5. Ask them for advice. Rather than telling them exactly what you want, ask for their advice. Estate agents have extensive local knowledge and usually enjoy sharing it.

6. Give viewing feedback. After each viewing, inform the agents what you did and did not like about the house. This will give them a clearer picture of exactly the sort of property you wish to purchase.

7. Keep in regular touch. Keep in regular contact with the estate agent, particularly after you have made an offer; call them to arrange access to the property for surveying, mortgage valuation, builders work assessment and so on. Always respond to their emails and telephone calls even if only to explain why you are not interested in a particular property. Call them every few days to let them know that you are still looking and ask if they have any news of new properties coming onto the market. If they don't hear from you, they will assume you are no longer looking.

8. Free up time to view properties. Good houses can sell very quickly, so make sure you are available to look at them. Do not miss a viewing without communication. It is rude and is likely to turn the agent against you. If you can't be available, get someone else to view the house on your behalf, someone who can accurately report to you after the visit.

9. Remember they are keen to sell. Although the agent works for the seller, and their commission gives them an incentive to obtain as high a price as possible, the bottom line is that they do want to close the deal and move on to the next. So they do have a slightly different agenda, which can move them to your side, namely that if they don't succeed in selling the property, they will receive nothing for all their efforts.

If they are the sole agent, they need to find a buyer fairly quickly, or the seller will put the property out to multiple agents.

If they are already one of multiple agents marketing the property, they will fear that if they don't seal the deal, another agent will.

This all means that agents can be more willing than the seller to accept a lower price, just to make sure they get a deal.

If a property is proving a little hard to shift, and is perhaps overpriced, the agent can effectively end up on your side, encouraging the seller to agree to your lower offer.

10. Be nice. This suggestion is not as obvious as is appears. Property investment can bring out the worst in people, with stressful timelines and conflicting interests. The vast majority of estate agents are decent people who have to work hard and long, in a very competitive market. So be nice to them. If you charm them, they might well respond favourably. If you have already purchased a house through them, stay in contact and send them little gifts (e.g. chocolates, wine, biscuits) so they'll remember to call you first when another house comes onto their books.

11. And if you don't have time and this is all too much… you can always use a sourcing agent, who will do this work on your behalf! But, if you do so, be prepared to pay a substantial fee for their services.

Here are some other members of your team:

Mortgage broker – offers advice about the various types of UK mortgages, from Buy-To-Let to First Time Buyer. Banks, building societies or estate agents can recommend mortgage brokers to you but I personally prefer to use an independent specialist mortgage broker who will scour the market to find for the right mortgage that suits my situation to ensure I will get the best deal.

Property solicitor / conveyancer – will ensure the smooth handling of your property transactions. This is essential to make sure your property purchases are completed in the timescale required to ensure a smooth transition.

Mentor or property investment coach – look for an experienced property investor who's 'done it and got the tee-shirt', who has achieved the results you are looking for, to increase your results and keep your property business on the right track.

Property accountant / tax expert – choose one who is also, ideally, an investor in property. An experienced accountant who specialises in the field of property will make sure that you can keep as much of your hard-earned profit as possible.

Project Manager – many new property acquisitions need some refurbishing to prepare them for sale or for new tenants. Depending on the extent of the work to be done, you could handle it yourself and save an outlay of capital. On the other hand, if you do still have your full time j.o.b., or if you own several properties, you may not have time to be a hands-on fixer upper. Or, you may simply not want to do this work yourself.

Will you be project managing the refurbishment works yourself or will you be appointing someone? Some letting agents offer this service as they already have a team of tradesmen they have worked with previously, with whose work they are familiar, and with whose quality they are satisfied.

You're still left with the task of overseeing and managing the work flow and quality.

Hiring a project manager does add to your costs, but could be worth it if this is a subject you don't know well, if it's a highly technical and multidiscipline project (e.g. adding a bathroom, building an extension, renovating a kitchen) or if you are preoccupied with other projects at the same time.

You can, of course, do this yourself if you have time. Some people actually enjoy this work and find it relaxing.

You could even appoint one trustworthy tradesperson for the job.

Letting agents – will be invaluable in helping you evaluate properties that you are considering purchasing or have purchased already. They can tell you what the best areas of town are and what the market rental would be for the properties that interest you.

Landlords and managers have to be "on call" 24/7. If there's an issue with plumbing, or if a tenant misses a rent payment, someone has to be ready, willing and able to jump in and manage the situation efficiently and within budget. It takes judgment and juggling. It's not for everyone.

Will you rent your property yourself or get a letting agent to do all the management for you? Many people prefer to handle the management on their own, although this may not be practical while you are still working at your full-time day job. There are emergencies and surprises that could require you to be available on a moment's notice, so when you're just getting started, you might prefer to outsource this important function.

Many independent agents offer excellent and personal service. Letting agents will charge a management fee for their services, which include making available a reliable and professional network of tradespeople, such as plumbers, electricians, builders, gardeners, handymen and other workers, for when things go wrong and to undertake any upgrades and improvements you may want to make in future.

Make sure you know more than your letting or managing agent to make sure you are benefiting from ethical, thorough, knowledgeable, responsible management and support.

Personal recommendation is a good way to find a suitable letting agency. Ask for advice from someone you know who has experience in dealing with local agents.

Choose a letting agent who is a member of the National Approved Letting Scheme or a professional organisation, such as the Association of Residential Letting Agents (ARLA), the National Association of Estate Agents (NAEA) or the Royal Institution of Chartered Surveyors (RICS). It is also a good idea to check whether they are registered with the Property Ombudsman. All are bound by a code of practice.

I also do my research online, read tenants' and landlords' reviews of letting agents' services. That gives me a short list of agents to contact, to ask about their offerings, to determine a possible fit.

Tradesmen – these are your builders, electricians, plumbers, tilers, decorators, handymen and gardeners, among others.

Reliable tradesmen will be essential to see to refurbishment works, routine maintenance, gas safety checks, electrical safety checks and Energy Performance Certificates (EPCs). If you use a managing agent, they will already have these teams in place, or you may have already used some different, trusted tradesmen before that you can use again. Always ask for a price for each job and agree on a timescale for the job, to ensure that everything is done within a set time frame, allowing your business to run more smoothly.

As you can see, a power team is vitally important to not only allow you to run your business smoothly, but it can also help to promote your business and lead to a referral network.

Delegate but don't relegate. Stay on top. Inspect what you expect.

Your Power Team is your knowledge base, your referral system and your production crew, but you are still in the driver's seat. Know the system yourself. Don't rely on others without verification and checking.

Remember that everyone on your team has their own axe to grind, their own profit to produce, their own agenda. So while, yes , your suppliers and service provider do have your interests at heart, they are there for their own "WHY".

Delegation does not mean relegation. Due diligence is absolutely yours to implement. Welcome the information and ideas and suggestions you get.

Then verify, validate, confirm, and protect.

Nothing personal – it's just business!

What about materials?

Now that you have the people in place, what about acquiring the materials? If you manage the purchase on your own, you're more likely to find deals, discounts, and opportunities to save. Chapter 7 has some information to help you.

Chapter 7
Market Value, Maths and Money

In Chapter 3, we covered the importance of preparing yourself before jumping in by investing in your personal development, educating yourself in all aspects of the property business and learning from people who have been there and already have successful property portfolios.

Before actually searching for property, sit down with a pen, paper and calculator to do real comparables to assess the cost of houses and the rent you are likely to achieve. You can easily get this information from the internet e.g. Rightmove, Zoopla among others.

MARKET VALUE is the key consideration as you shop around for property. It's not difficult to surf the net and locate "comparables" – other houses with similar characteristics – to measure the fairness of the asking price where you're looking. But average pricing generates average returns.

Price too high? You'll impact your cash flow plan, and your gain when you eventually decide to sell.

Price too low? This might sound appealing, but why is your property below the norm? Are there easements, liens, zoning, structural or other concerns? Did the existing owner get promoted out of the country and is looking for a quick close? Or was this the site of a murder?

If you're handy, if you're proactive, if you're confident you can bring the place up to standard and still show positive financials, you may have discovered the "diamond in the rough".

I learned that I don't want to have the most fabulous property on the street so I don't want to overdo the upgrades and the fixes. The additional expense is not likely to result in a rent significantly higher than the "going rate" for the area. From a value appreciation perspective, you can gain leverage from the neighbouring properties if they are better than yours. That's a much better strategy than being the high end place, and having the other properties limit the potential of yours.

And of course, it's also a matter of budget. A HUGE matter of budget!

What is a good deal in property investment?

We all love bargains; hence professional investors look for houses below market value (BMV) as profit can be achieved from day 1 when the deal is closed. Nobody deliberately chooses to sell a house for less than it's worth but, in some cases, there are a number of reasons why people will sell below the actual value. These are 'motivated sellers' who need to sell quickly because of various reasons such as:-

1. Work relocation or they are emigrating abroad
2. Probate so they can share out the funds to the beneficiaries of a deceased person's estate
3. Repossession, so the mortgage company can sell the property to recover the debt it is owed
4. Debt issues, financial difficulties or redundancy; sellers might have to dispose of the property in order to avoid bankruptcy, repossession or to settle outstanding debts

5. Divorce; it could be that a couple hate each other so much that they don't care how much money they lose so long as the other one loses too!
6. Retiring, tired, or landlord selling their excess property portfolio
7. Housing Associations selling off their old stock houses to fund new builds
8. Councils selling properties that have been empty for several years, whose owners are deceased or unknown, so they can be refurbished and used again, instead of becoming derelict or being occupied by squatters

Do the Maths

Buy to Let (BTL) lenders typically want the rent to cover 125% of the mortgage payments. The best BTL mortgage rates come with large arrangement fees so it's best to shop around. It's a great idea to talk to a few independent mortgage brokers who can talk you through what deals are available and help you weigh which one is right for you. At the same time, you should do your own research so you can go into conversations armed with some knowledge of what sort of mortgages you can expect. We all have our opinion on what return to look for in buy to let property investment. What I've learned and am applying in all my BTL purchases is:-

- the achievable rental income will be sufficient to cover payment for mortgage interest at 5% or 6%, plus the lender's margin based on borrowing at 75% loan to value (LTV), ongoing maintenance cost, managing agent's fee, insurance, licences among others (and if applicable, ground rent and service charges), giving a net cash flow of at least 10% (although, in some cases, 8% is acceptable as this is also a better interest rate than the banks or building society) and

- check out the properties in the area that have been sold in the last 6 months and do comparables.

Case Study 1

The illustration below uses the exact figures sent to me by a sourcing agent for a 2 bedroom apartment with a 125 year lease:-

Financial Breakdown based on 2 bedroom apartment;

This example is based on a 75% LTV (loan to value) buy to let mortgage; the figures may vary depending on the finance you obtain. **Your** mortgage broker can advise on the best product for you.

*Estimated Market Value**	*£220,000*
Discounted price	*£193,575*
Instant Equity	*£26,425*
Mortgage @ 75% LTV	*£145,181*
Mortgage payments @ 2.89%	*£350pcm*
Current rental	*£825pcm*
Surplus Income after Mortgage	*£475pcm*
Costs	
Finder's Fee (inc VAT)	*£6,969*
Stamp Duty	*£1,372*
Total Costs	*£6,372*
Deposit Required (75% LTV)	*£48,394*
Overall Outlay	*£54,766*

** The Estimated Market Value is based on our own due diligence which can include the price of sold properties in the area, comparable properties currently on the market and estate agents' interviews.*
Any legal/mortgage fees have not been added to the table.

As this is a leasehold property, there is also a ground rent of £395 per year and a Service Charge of approximately £850 per year which hasn't been included in the agent's calculation.

My own financial due diligence calculation based on the given figures above as follows:-

	Agent	My calculation
Estimated Market Value*	£220,000	£220,000
Discounted price	**£193,575**	**£193,575**
Instant Equity	**£26,425**	**£26,425**
Mortgage @ 75% LTV Mortgage payments @ 2.89%	£145,181 £350pcm	£145,181 £350pcm (although realistically, I would always allow at least a 5% mortgage payment i.e. £650 PCM) £33 Ground rent £71 Service Charge £99 Managing agent's fee @10% + VAT £83 Other expenses @ 10% £636 total expenses (or £891 if mortgage is at 5%)
Current rental **Surplus Income after Mortgage**	£825pcm **£475pcm (a)**	£825pcm **£189pcm (a) – Surplus after expenses and mortgage** Or if mortgage is at 5%, this will give a deficit of **–£66**
Costs		
Finder's Fee (inc VAT) Stamp Duty	£6,969 £1,372	£6,969 £1,372 £1,000 legal fees £500 broker fees £500 survey fee £500 miscellaneous expenses
Total Costs	£6,372	**£10,841**
Deposit Required (75% LTV)	£48,394	£48,394
Overall Outlay **ROI [(a x 12) / (b)]**	**£54,766 (b)** 10%	**£59,235 (b)** – excluding refurb cost 4%

The original (sourcing agent) figures showed a 10% return, within my requirement.

According to my own calculations, after taking into account the sourcing fee, service charges, professional fees, managing agent fees and other expenses, it worked out that the ROI (return on investment) is only 4%, not the 10% they were claiming.

Based on my own financial due diligence, I walked away from this deal as it did not meet my criteria and expectations.

SOME LOSSES = THE COST OF DOING BUSINESS

Before I buy any property, I get a survey done, I pay solicitors to do a search, and I get as much information up front as I possibly can. If I find the information meets my criteria, it's a win. If not, not so much!

That said, I had to back out of at least 3 places that interested me. And in all 3 cases, without the information provided by professionals, I might have dived in – and lost big-time! The incidentals of paying the professionals saved me from making a much bigger mistake in the long run.

Case Study 2 – my deal

Property type: 3 bedroom 2 reception room, freehold property

Estimated Market Value			£80,000
Purchase Price Agreed			£67,000
Deposit @ 25% LTV		£16,750	
Refurbishment, etc cost	£10,000		
Broker fee	£500		
Legals	£500		
		£11,000	
Purchase cost		£27,750	

Rent pcm (per calendar month)		£525
Less Expenses:		
Mortgage @ 5%	£209	
Management fee @ 10%	£52.50	
Other expenses e.g. insurance etc @ 10%	£52.50	
Total expenses		£314
Net Income pcm		**£211**
ROI (£211 x 12 / £27,750)		**9.12%**

The above deal meets my criteria, so I bought the house. In fact, the mortgage interest rate I acquired is below 5%, therefore the actual net ROI on this deal over 10%.

FISCAL AND PHYSICAL DUE DILIGENCE:

You can only find out the physical defects once a survey has been completed. Then you need to assess the defects and determine the costs to refurbish to your own standards.

After doing the sums and refurbishment costs, after projecting achievable rents and finding the figures unsuitable, expenses like survey fees, solicitor, search fees, etc., I chose to walk away. Be prepared to incur expenses even if you then need to walk. This is the cost of doing business.

In each situation, I had to redo my sums, explore every option to generate positive cash flow, and leave when the numbers didn't work out in my favour.

The sums helped me remain objective, even in the face of emotion.

Once you have calculated the mortgage rate and the rent you are likely to receive, make sure you calculate the other expenses you will need to factor in (see Chapter 8 for details).

WHERE WILL THE MONEY COME FROM?

In my case, I was able to finance my property purchases by using my savings that were not generating a good return and angel investors.

There are several other ways of financing your BTL property through traditional lenders, like banks, mortgage brokers and bridging loan companies.

But if your investment is 'interesting' – has great cash flow – and potential for appreciation in capital value, you may find investors and money sources looking for you!

Your money – Self Financing

Review your finances, ideally with your professional advisors. You'll want to reassess your monthly income, your monthly outgoings and what you have left after deducting them. Whatever's left is your savings.

What about your own savings?

Are you a saver? Do your savings earn favourable returns? Will your property investments generate a better return? If so, this is the way to go.

The thing about property is to figure out the best way to hold onto it on your terms. After the initial financial bite, there are the ongoing expenses, repairs, maintenance, vacancies and other obligations that will cost money. To minimize the impact of these, do even more homework up front. Sharpen your pencil, grab a calculator, do some research and negotiate wherever possible to provide the best possible cash flow.

Other people's money:

Although there's no shortage of money in the world, having the right amount at the right time is a challenge for many. Lenders, partners, even family members and other money people are cautious about where their money is placed, how secure and solid the concept is, and when they'll get their ROI, i.e. their exit strategy.

Debt-service ratio is a formula applied to the balance between how much money you qualify to receive, based on how much money you are likely to be able to repay.

So it should be no surprise that although the obvious first resource is the bank, their requirements are the most stringent, and their policies are the least flexible.

To leverage your interest and your plans, you likely will want to explore less obvious sources of finance.

Partnerships have their share of challenges over the long term. However, if your life partner has the wherewithal, why not consider joint venturing with someone who already loves you? Or partnering with other investors, whose credit potential may provide greater leverage and opportunity than you'd have individually?

And then there's **Angel Finance.** People with lots of money are often people with lots of responsibility, lots of activity, and lots of interest in finding newer ways to place their money for even more growth and higher returns. They are always open to interesting deals, maximum leverage, and strategies for growth. You can locate these people quite easily, on social media, online, through networking and by participating in the various events I've mentioned throughout this book.

You may think it's all about money. But to get to the money, it's really about people!

WHERE TO FIND INVESTORS

Start with people who already love you, like family and friends. That said, though, money is a delicate subject for many, so remember, it's a business venture. Treat it as such, with property discussion and documentation – and honour your commitments.

Not all husbands are handy – until they want to be! – Mine is an ANGEL!

My husband never wanted to be saddled with another mortgage debt, having paid off the loan on our first home and then purchased our current home outright with the proceeds of its sale. He was determined that our children's home should not be used as security for my venture, so there was no question of raising money by mortgaging it. In fact, he didn't want any type of involvement in my shenanigans. He was willing to accept what I was doing, but he was not going to do any of the "heavy lifting" – or any lifting at all, for that matter.

Then he saw that my work was starting to pay off. It was working, and he was becoming intrigued.

My husband is a semi-retired, self-employed private tutor and writer of military historical games. While he writes articles on his computer, he often has the television on in the background.

He started watching property shows and became interested in the auction and property programmes – such the BBC series Homes Under The Hammer – when he started to realize the tremendous potential of my investment approach.

I'm happy to say that, at this time, my husband is actually one of the angel investors in my property business.

So it's ironic that before, when I was very hesitant and afraid to get a mortgage, I had to assure him that everything would be in my own name and that I would do all the work…

And now here he is, ready and willing to get into it with me. He came to my BTL houses where he helped out with the refurbishments and now he seems to be happy with this property business idea – but there's still no way he would take out a mortgage on our family home!

Earlier I mentioned that, when it came to developing housing in the Philippines, my mother became my joint venture partner. This was partly for the ROI, but mainly for the vision of helping people in our homeland.

It's the same for other contacts. They may be willing to invest just because they know you and trust you. But truly, there's a financial return they'll be expecting on their investment.

Trust and money are strange bedfellows. Protect both!

Sourcing Refurbishment Materials Cheaply

Refurbishment can incur ongoing and escalating costs.

You can control many aspects of the cost of your refurbishment: for example, by sourcing the materials yourself at discount. You can find a tremendous range of materials options, prices, composition, quality and availability…

How do you get materials, furniture and fixtures at discount or even for free?

Here are some tips:-

- Get a trade card – you can usually get goods at discounted trade price
- Buy items on sale – basic good quality materials are fine, as you're not going to live in the house anyway
- Car boot sales – you'll be surprised what you can find at a boot sale, some second hand for your investment property, some new that you may want for your own home
- Use the Freecycle or Gumtree websites to advertise your own surplus items and to obtain free stuff. I once managed to source high quality bathroom and kitchen tiles, that I would never have considered buying for one of my rental properties, by this method. It costs me nothing, because people are usually happy to get rid of their excess materials, at no expense to themselves and in exchange for minimal effort, knowing they will be recycled and put to good use. As they say, 'someone's junk is somebody else's treasure'.
- Join organisations such as the NLA (National Landlord Association) or NLPG (National Landlord Property Group). There is usually a subscription fee to join these groups, but such fees are tax deductible. In addition, they also have tradesmen on their lists who have track records you can verify, and many offer discounts to members. Being a member of NLA is also recognised by the local council, so that you can secure a discount when you apply for a HMO (House of Multiple Occupation) licence.

KEEP TRACK

In addition to being thorough and detailed, you have to be organized. With so many numbers, figures, documents, confirmations, invoices, receipts, accounts, revenues and numbers flying in and out of your accounting system, it can be problematic if you rely on "shoebox accounting", where you toss every receipt into a box and go through it – or hand it over to an accountant – at the end of the year for tax purposes.

Actually you should maintain an ongoing record of your financial ins and outs to protect yourself from unforeseen surprises when it comes to the year-end.

Above all else, the tax department requires you to pay your share.

This is where your financial advisor or accountant will be extremely important. Get them to help you structure your accounts to avoid confusion when it's time to do your tax return.

Chapter 8
Taking (the right) Action at the right TIME (STRATEGIES)

To have satisfaction, you must also have action. There is 'action' in the word satisfaction.

Not just any action – calculated action.

I have always wanted to own houses that I could see myself living in. If I can satisfy myself, I can satisfy the kind of tenants I want to have in my houses. Some owners just do basic upgrades and maintenance. Then they attract a lower level of tenant who sometimes trashes the place.

Will you be investing to achieve immediate regular passive income? Or are you planning for capital growth? Or both?

If you plan wisely, you could combine strategies for a worry-free cash flow: invest for immediate passive income in the short term, even while also anticipating property price increases in the longer term.

The capital growth strategy is best achieved in large, thriving cities like London, but you will need a lot of cash to put down as a deposit.

For example, up in the north of the United Kingdom, properties are considerably cheaper than in London or the south. A nurse working in a London hospital will struggle to rent a decent apartment; a four-hour train ride north, in Sunderland, nurses can afford to buy their own houses. This means that a smaller cash deposit is needed in the north, while the percentage rental return on your investment is quicker and usually higher than can be achieved in London. On the other hand, property appreciation is a tad slow in these regions and can take several years longer than in the major centres.

REFURBISHMENT, a major consideration in time and money

There's a fine balance between fixing up and renovating. The range varies by the demographic of the area, the standards of the places near yours and the expectations of the type of tenant you hope to attract to rent your property.

I always want to find someone like myself, who takes pride in their space, who will take care of the residence as if they owned it, – and of course, a tenant who is responsible and reliable and can afford to pay the desired rent, with increases as the years go by.

That's why I make it a point to stay in the location for at least a night or two. Then whatever needs adjusting, fixing, replacing or repairing can be handled in one concentrated time frame and the result is fresh, clean and people-ready.

Family Houses

I always want to let my properties as quickly as possible. That means I have to complete the refurbishment as soon as I can and get the adverts out there as soon as possible.

What I've also learned, though, is that if you choose the right house in the right location, where there is more demand for housing than there is supply of properties, prospective tenants will come to you.

We have already touched on the importance of finding the right property suitable for the right tenant, in an area of high demand. That's both to attract the best tenants, and also to do so quickly. Void units are costly!

Therefore, it's always a rush when I first purchase a house, or when I'm "between tenants", to get the place cleaned up, freshened up or even totally refurbished in time to get new people in. That could require minor fixes as well as much more significant work.

The longer it takes for the refurbishment, the longer it takes for me to locate a great tenant and for money to start coming my way. So when I do my maths, I allow for 6 weeks' time to refurbish, regardless of the depth of the job, from "buff and fluff" to a full refurbishment.

HMO

In the United Kingdom, houses in multiple occupation (HMO) are also known as bedsits, flatlets and shared houses. An HMO is a property rented out to at least 3 people who are not from one household (e.g. a family) but share facilities like toilet, bathroom or kitchen with other tenants. For more information, visit https://www.gov.uk/private-renting/houses-in-multiple-occupation.

In the case of student HMOs there's a season that starts and ends on a fixed schedule. That means that you can pre-arrange the plan, the team, the resources and even the money to pay for any clean-ups and refurbishments, all to take place right after the end of the university or college year.

In the case of HMOs let to itinerant workers, it is extremely unlikely that the whole property will ever be completely empty, so it will be difficult to undertake renovation other that on a room-by-room basis.

Even then, it's a competitive market and you'll want your adverts to start promoting your place early, certainly before your competitors!

For BtL, it's a matter of void time between acquiring the place and having it tenanted. This idle time can become very costly if your refurbishment takes much longer than predicted.

Planning is the key.

Many people who are experienced in refurbishment will advise you to budget for twice the money and twice the time. Can you afford either?

As Abraham Lincoln said, "If you have 9 hours to chop down a cherry tree, use 8 hours to sharpen your axe!"

CASE STUDY:

My very first refurbishment was in a high-demand area. Even while the work was in progress, I started receiving inquiries from passers-by who had seen my builders at work, about when it would be available for rent. Location, location, location. We were definitely in the right one!

When my managing agent placed an advertisement for the property even while the refurbishment was still underway, I asked if there had been any inquiries. He was not keen on the one or two he'd received because the people sounded like they were social housing (LHA) tenants, and I wanted to let to a working family or professionals.

The managing agent had even taken some photographs, but the quality was not up to my own expectations.

As soon as the refurbishment works were complete, I took pictures of my own, and that very same evening I placed an advert on Gumtree.

When I told the letting manager what I had done, he warned me that it wasn't likely to work. He said that there were lots of housing benefit tenants who frequented that site, and that the standard of applicant would be lower than I wanted.

Within 24 hours my phone started ringing – and ringing, and ringing.

Yes, there were some LHA tenants. But there were also several professional tenants. So many, in fact, that I had to filter out those who did not sound like the sort of people I wanted as tenants.

I reached out by email and lo and behold! I actually found a tenant through Gumtree!

So I proved my letting agent wrong and within one week, I found the tenant myself.

That showed me that by doing the job myself, I was able to get better results than the people who said they do this work on a regular basis.

Then I followed the same principles on my next deal – and my next one.

So if you know what you're doing and are learning from other people, you can't go wrong.

For my second house, we never had to advertise in the press or on the internet at all. Instead, during the refurbishment, I asked the letting agent to put up his sign at the front of the property even while the works were still ongoing. And again, people came by to list their names as potential tenants.

Buying Strategies:
Don't skip any steps.
I know. I tried, and I got caught.

CASE STUDY

So there I was, studying and searching, when I saw a property I liked, got excited and made an offer. It was accepted. I felt so proud of myself.

I did my homework as I'd been taught, and I spent money on solicitors, the broker, a survey, and all the other preliminaries. I did my sums a time or two. And after running up fees for these services, I redid my sums. But, in the end, after all the preparatory analysis and assessment, I re-analyzed the project and finally backed out.

When I first saw that place, I thought it would work for a working professional. But after making a further visit to the property, I concluded that the fact the only bathroom had no window and so was probably inadequately ventilated, in addition to being somewhat claustrophobic, was not likely to appeal to potential tenants. I had also contemplated having a single storey extension, within permitted development so it would not require planning permission, to increase the ground floor area to create an open plan kitchen/dining room. Closer examination of the small yard to the rear of the property, however, revealed a manhole cover and a drain underneath the site of the proposed extension – moving those would be both costly and time-consuming. Through further research, I discovered that there were a lot more families in the area, many of whom were housing benefit tenants, which meant that my target tenants were going to avoid that district.

Yes, my training and support saved me from going forward and making an even bigger error. But had I finished the program before jumping into the investment, I probably would have dismissed this property based on the asking price.

You can do it relatively quickly if you put your mind to it. But you need to know the rules – and follow them!

I had jumped in without really digging, without quadruple checking – and in the process, I lost money on those professional fees. Had I completed the course, I could have saved myself the stress, the aggravation – and the money! But the learning was invaluable.

Like Arthur Wellesley (the future Duke of Wellington) in his first campaign in the Low Countries in 1794, "I learned what not to do, and that is always useful."

I shall not make that mistake again!

WHAT STRATEGY BEST SUITS YOU?

My focus on immediate cash flow addressed my need to replace my employment income.

There are many other property investment strategies, long- and short-term, every scope, with different timelines and risk levels. These are outside the parameters of my initial property program. Buy to Flip, Rent to Rent, lease options, commercial and residential concepts, buying at auction…all interesting, but not for me yet.

Don't buy blind.

AUCTION CASE STUDY:

I was drawn to attend an auction when I saw the very, very low prices for their units. I attended just out of curiosity. And while there, I came very close to buying.

Luckily I recognized the husband of one of my course-trainers. He had more experience and information about this type of property. Through him I found out that these are more suited for corporate pension plans because they are long-term investments. The purchase would be just the freehold reversion, not the right to occupy the actual house, which was tenanted. If I bought the freehold, I would still have to pay for the building's insurance and be responsible for the maintenance of the fabric of the building itself!

Once I learned the details, I saw that this type of investment, at this time, was not really for me. It would take years before I'd be able to generate income – and my immediate strategy is immediate income.

Being in London, high energy, professional auctioneers generating emotional reactions and excitement was not my style. Actually, with all that hype, properties were selling for much higher than the asking prices – even double in some cases!

Subsequently I attended an auction course. Armed with this new knowledge, I am more prepared to attend another property auction in future.

You have to do your research. My revelation (reminder, actually) was to do my homework before ever stepping into the auction hall. When I'm ready to reconsider this strategy in future, I will visit the house first, do background checks and as much due diligence as possible before ever placing a bid.

One step in the right direction is worth a hundred years of thinking about it!

STRATEGIES:

What strategy would you like to apply when investing in Buy-To-Let (BTL) property? Are you looking for ongoing passive income right away? Or are you investing for long-term capital appreciation as the value of the property increases? Both strategies are possible.

My personal choice is to invest for passive income, although your needs may be different. For me, regular income enabled me to leave my employee status as soon as the net rental income generated from my property portfolio equalled my salary from my employment.

1. Income or
2. Capital growth

Income from BUY to LET (BTL)

With a BTL strategy, you collect monthly rental income from your tenants. The rent you receive depends on the type of property you have, its location, the local demand and the demographic of your tenants, who may be students, working professionals, families, DSS (Department of Social Security) people or housing benefits tenants.

Even with the best planning and the greatest tenants, surprises do surface, and you need to be prepared to address them. What about periods when you may not have a tenant in your property? How about any redecorating and repairs in order to attract great tenants in the first place?

Apart from the cost of buying the property itself, there are other acquisition costs to cover such as:-

- Mortgage arrangement fees
- Valuation / Survey fees
- Broker fees if you are using one
- Legal fees for conveyancing etc.
- Stamp duty
- Building or refurbishment costs

Once you acquire the property, you also acquire regular expenses such as:-

- Mortgage interest (not capital repayments)
- Managing and/or letting agent fees
- Landlord Building and Contents Insurance
- Annual safety checks – gas, electrics, fire safety equipment
- General building maintenance
- Repairs
- Property Management (unless you are doing the work yourself)
- HMO (House of Multiple Occupation) license fee – payable in some areas if you have multiple occupancy rooms to let

- For furnished properties, a 'wear and tear' allowance of 10% of the annual rental income
- Accounting fees if you are using an accountant
- Income tax on any profits you make on rental property
- Council Tax
- Utilities – water, gas, electricity

In the UK, even if the house is unoccupied, or currently being refurbished, council tax and utilities must be paid by you, the landlord. The quicker you let your house, the better, so you can cover these and other expenses.

I only buy ***freehold*** *properties, so certain expenses such as service charges and ground rents for leasehold properties are omitted from the above list.*

And when you sell the property there are other fees, such as:-

- Capital Gains tax
- Estate agent's commission
- Legal fees
- Mortgage early redemption penalty fee (usually incurred if you sell before the end of two years' ownership)

It's extremely important to keep detailed records and a tight control of your costs. Run the numbers carefully and accurately. Factor in at least one month of rental void into your calculations to minimize the impact of this if and when your property is vacant for a time. It's always safer to over-estimate expenses and to plan accordingly.

Make sure you keep all receipts and invoices. If you make a loss on the rental property, you can carry the loss forward to offset against profits from the property in future years. For more information on tax, go to www.hmrc.gov.uk

Put off with the expenses so far? Don't be. So long as 'the maths' sum is positive, achieving at least 10% return on your investment, you're okay (at least that's what works for me). If you have an HMO, you could achieve an even higher return on your investment. And then, you can repeat the same process for your next property venture.

Capital Growth

One of the money-making strategies through property letting is capital growth, also known as capital appreciation. This is when a property increases in value over time. Capital growth is the amount of money you make when you sell.

Of course, the value of a property can go down as well as up, so the local conditions surrounding your property have a big effect. And your reliance upon market timing is another concern.

Your timing plans can contribute to your best choice of property to buy, i.e. on how long you plan on keeping your investment intact. You want to be able to sell when the right time comes for you to liquidate.

What is your timeline like?

Many property investors have a fixed-term 'buy and hold' strategy in mind, e.g. for 5, 10 or 20 years.

Timing can be a significant factor in the amount. Your investment will only be worth what someone is willing to pay AT THAT TIME.

Local experts can sometimes tell you about off-market property, new developments, town regeneration and up and coming areas, which can all result in property values increasing over a specific number of years.

Capital growth strategies are suitable for particular longer-term objectives, like retirement, ultimate family support, university fees for children, or even balancing the increasing cost of living over time.

Once you've found the "best" property you may also find competition from other investors, which can push the price up. Even so, although you may not find a 'bargain', if you've researched and explored all of the options, and if you see the property providing you with a monthly income, and anticipate positive capital growth in five, 10, or 20 years' time, you're on the road to freedom.

HMOs: dream or nightmare?

An HMO (house of multiple occupation) is a property rented out to at least 3 people who are not from one household (e.g. a family) but share facilities like the bathroom and kitchen. It's sometimes called a 'house share'.

Your property is defined as a large HMO if all of the following apply:

- it's rented to 5 or more people who form more than 1 household
- it's at least 3 storeys high
- tenants share a toilet, bathroom or kitchen facilities

Most areas in UK require that the landlord have a licence when renting out a large HMO. Even if your property is smaller and rented to fewer people, you may still need a licence, depending on the area. Check with your local council.

Although the return on an HMO can be significantly higher than a more traditional family BTL, the work involved in maintaining and managing these multi-tenant facilities is much harder.

Students who occupy an HMO normally do so on a ten-month contract, commencing with the academic year in September and running until the end of June with an option to renew.

It's helpful to understand the timeframes of your prospective tenants. In the UK, A level (senior school) examination results are not published until mid-August, after which the students start looking for places to live in for September when they start University. Second-year students start looking for accommodation earlier, since they are already enrolled at the university, and many stay at the same place as the year before.

After the students leave for summer holiday, the property will be empty and ready for refurbishment. Since the academic year ends in early summer, any repairs and refurbishments need to done during the summer and completed by the start of the new academic year in September. The earlier you can complete the upgrades and repairs, the more likely you are to attract the best tenants.

At that point, before the next rental season begins, the managing agent is supposed to freshen up the place for viewings by prospective tenants.

"Supposed to", in our case, meant "did not".

CASE STUDY:

It was my first HMO. When the tenants left, my husband and I went there to experience what it was like to live in that space, to find out what was working and what was not.

At the same time, although my managing agent should have done the clear out, check out, making sure that the house had been left in tip top condition and documenting any breakages and damage to charge back to the existing tenants, this had not happened.

The managing agents had not done their job.

Had we relied on distant communication and off-site management, we'd be in trouble today.

As it happened, since this was my first HMO, 3.5 hours from my home, I decided to go there and see things first-hand.

My husband and I stayed in the property for four nights to get a sense of the quality of life we were offering to our tenants, while also making sure we fixed whatever needed doing to raise the standard of the place to meet the standards of higher quality renters. As landlords, we wanted to make sure we could attract and satisfy serious, qualified renters.

What we found was horrific.

First we located a 20-litre bin of smelly rubbish, then a big container full of rotting food, a broken chair, and two broken vacuum cleaners, none of which had been ever reported to us. And of course there was the general condition of the property, which needed refreshing and cleaning.

So while we had planned to spend part of our travelling time exploring the area, I actually ended up cleaning and painting shelves and cupboards throughout the property.

We were shocked – but also relieved – we had chosen to go this route.

We might never have known, had we not set aside plenty of time to dig deeper, roll up our sleeves and do what needed to be done instead of relying on telephone updates from the so-called managing agent.

I tried the washing machine. It didn't work. It made me wonder if the previous student tenants had ever done any laundry! Whether they did or not, nobody ever mentioned that there was anything wrong with these appliances.

They should have reported the faulty equipment. Maybe they were the ones who had actually broken it!

Either way, this will remain a mystery. Nobody told us, even though we were paying 10% of our rent plus VAT for management services. Actually, the managing agents were charging the students for cleaning, so we did not have to pay for it, – but it appeared that this was never done.

As we worked away, we listed all the things the managing agent had not done, and they said they would now take care of them. Had we not gone, we'd have remained in the dark, paying for services that were needed but not been provided, and, more important, marketing a substandard place.

During our stay, we found that one room needed redecorating. Because of condensation, we had to strip the walls and repaper. We also had to paint a fire door in order to get back up to standard for the HMO inspection. They would only give us our 5-year license to operate an HMO after confirming that everything was to their satisfaction.

And of course the walls were badly marked up.

And we kept finding more and more things needing fixing.

For example, the sealant that had been used in the kitchen was not the correct mould-resistant type that you can buy from any DIY shop. As a result, it had developed unsightly mould, and I had to physically scrape it from the kitchen and from the bathrooms. Then I replaced all the grout in the kitchen and finally got the management agent to complete the work.

The previous landlord had relied on the managing agent to do everything. In fact, before I purchased, I was told that the landlord had not been there for two years. That meant that the previous landlord had never actually done a thorough check around the house years before.

Our investigation was the first to reveal these problems.

And now, after working so hard for almost a week, we were confident that everything looked spanking new, up to standard, welcoming and ready for a more serious, more responsible tenant.

One great point is that after our work was done, early in the season, with the renovation complete, the managing agent could start arranging viewings earlier than others, to get an edge on finding great tenants for next year. No surprise that the best houses go fastest!

What to ask the estate agent when buying and viewing a property

Estate agents are legally bound to tell you the truth about the property so you need to make sure you ask the right questions to find out what the real situation is.

1. Why is the owner selling?
The agent doesn't have to answer, but if you're lucky they might hint at the circumstances. You might find out the owner is desperate to sell, perhaps because work is taking them overseas, and so would accept a lower price.

2. How long has the property been on the market?
If the house has been on the market a long time (more than three months), ask the agent why they think it isn't selling. Does it have defects or problems that other people have discovered, but you haven't? Is it just overpriced? A long time on the market may well result in the seller being willing to accept an offer below the asking price.

3. How old is the property? Is it in a conservation area? Is it listed? If yes, what grade is it?
Not only is this nice to know anyway, but the upkeep of older houses, particularly listed, is often more expensive. If you buy a listed property you will be severely restricted as to what you can do both to the outside and, in some cases, to the inside too. If the property is in a conservation area you should find out exactly what restrictions apply before making an offer.

4. How long have the sellers owned the property or lived there?
If they are selling or moving out after a short period, it is important to find out why. Do they have bad tenants? Noisy or unpleasant neighbours?

5. Is there anything that you would want to know about the house if you were buying?
The big fear if you are buying is that you could be missing some major negative factor that others know about. For example: are the next door neighbours the family from hell? People have been known to move into the homes of convicted mass-

murderers without knowing – and you can bet they wish they had known before!

If you have any doubts about a house, ask next-door neighbours or local shop keepers for their opinions of the property, the area and the neighbours.

6. Exactly what is included in the sale?

Is a garage included? What about garden sheds or greenhouses? Fixtures and fittings – kitchen units, built in ovens and hobs, bathroom suites and light fittings, for example – are normally included in a sale, unless specifically exempted in the contract, but freestanding kitchen appliances, furniture, curtains and light bulbs are not. Exactly where does the boundary lie? Make sure you know and see exactly what you are getting. Your solicitor will normally check this out for you when you agree to the sale before exchange of contract.

7. Has the property repeatedly changed hands?

You can check this out beforehand by visiting the Land Registry website. You should be alerted to serious problems if the property has frequently changed hands. Find out why previous owners sold the house or moved out.

8. How did the agent decide on an asking price?

A good agent will provide you with their justifications for the asking price. Sometimes, they might tell you that they think the seller is overvaluing the house. You should, however, do your own due diligence and check comparable houses in the immediate area that have been sold recently, so you have a good idea what prices similar properties have achieved.

9. What is the minimum price the seller will accept?

Don't hesitate to ask what the seller's bottom figure is, and whether this is negotiable, as it can save you thousands. Estate agents will often give you an indication – it is in their interest to make a sale, even at a lower price, because if they don't sell, they don't get paid any commission.

10. What offers have they had so far?
The agent will most likely tell you if there have been other offers, but not how much they were. But again, they have a great incentive to get a price agreed, so might drop some pretty heavy hints in whispered tones. If you can discover what other offers have been made, it will obviously be easier to know what you should offer.

11. Is the property tenanted or the seller living there? When are they vacating the house?
Have the sellers or tenant already found another house? Is the seller a tired landlord trying to get rid of their unwanted property portfolio? If so, they are probably keen to sell as quickly as possible to ensure that their own purchase is completed successfully. Otherwise, if you have to wait till they find somewhere else, it adds to the uncertainty, and you could end up in a long chain that might fall through.

12. Can you speak directly to the sellers?
Agents generally hate this – it is their job to negotiate – but they can't stop you speaking to the sellers, which can be the best thing you do. It can give you a much better feel for the house – ask them the best and worst points.

13. Have any major works been carried out?
If so, are you able to have a look at the relevant planning and building control consents? It would be awful if you bought your dream home only to find out you have to knock half of it down because the appropriate permissions had not been obtained for recently completed work, or the work had not been completed in accordance with building regulations. Beware the enthusiastic

amateur DIY enthusiast who has made substantial alterations to his property! When my husband bought his first house, the owner had 'decorated' the open-plan living room by fixing strips of black wood on the walls and ceiling to make the interior resemble a sixteenth century Tudor dwelling. When these timbers were removed, my husband discovered that a load-bearing wall had been removed, but not properly supported; neither had the kitchen chimney breast! Three rigid steel joists (RSJs) had to be installed, at a cost of over 10% of the purchase price. In such cases, a structural survey is a very good idea.

14. Can you move the furniture and have a peek under the rugs?

It is not unknown to hide cracks in the wall with furniture or cover up floor problems with rugs. So ensure you look thoroughly. Remember that a surveyor will not always do so.

15. Is there central heating? How old is the boiler?

Boiler replacement can be expensive. Ask if the boiler has been regularly serviced, and ask for the latest gas certificate. It's always good to allow for a new boiler/central heating replacement when negotiating the price.

16. How new or how sturdy are the drains and guttering?

Replacing drainage is a very expensive pain. If it is raining, seize the opportunity to check that nothing is leaking.

17. What can they tell you about the local neighbourhood?

What are the local schools like? What is the crime rate like? How good are local transport links? Where is the nearest petrol station? While it is a good idea to see what the estate agent has to say, make sure you do some independent research as well.

Chapter 9
Putting It All Together

There are many aspects to property investment. As such, you will be needing the most up-to-date information and advice. Before you actually buy a property, you need to quadruple check that it's a sound investment. It's no good falling in love with a house if there is no rental market in the area or the rent will not cover the mortgage and other expenses.

Align yourself with qualified professionals before signing anything. Another consideration is that rules and regulations can be different from neighbourhood to neighbourhood, so make sure your information is local in nature.

So, you have found the right location, identified the house you want to buy, confirmed that you have at least 25% deposit to put down based on the asking price, or have found an angel or joint venture partner/s ready to help you financially, chosen a mortgage broker and solicitor or conveyancer recommended to you (NOTE: If it's the estate agent's recommendation, it will likely be commission-based advice and will cost you); what next?

Financial stuff

"Love the numbers first and the property second"
– Ethan, Author at MortgageIntellectual.com

There are several ways of financing your property.

If you have lots of money at your fingertips, you could buy for cash.

More likely, though, you'll be obtaining a mortgage with the help of a mortgage broker. You can even do this yourself by going straight to a bank or building society mortgage adviser – but will then be limited to the financial products of that particular institution.

I prefer to use an independent mortgage broker who researches the various mortgage lenders for the best deals on interest repayments and fees.

Before you begin your search, it is a good idea to get your mortgage AIP (Agreement in Principle) to help speed up the process when you're ready to make an offer to buy. An AIP is also sometimes called a Decision in Principle, or DIP. Your independent mortgage broker will normally arrange to get this for you.

Essentially, an AIP is a credit report search that is pre-approved, subject to finding a property, property valuation and providing the lender with any supporting documentation. Your mortgage broker will determine how much you can borrow so you can start fully informed of your options.

Time for the offer. How much?

All properties are different, and in the end **a property is only worth what someone is prepared to pay for it.** *That means that it is basically impossible to generate a perfect "right" price for what an individual property is worth.*

- Keep your eye on the local market trends. Are prices falling, or rising; if so, how fast? What's driving the change?
- Get to know the area. Do comparables. Find out how much other identical or similar houses in the same area or street have sold for recently. You can do your research online by looking at various websites, such as the Land Registry, Rightmove, Zoopla, Primelocation and Nethouseprices.
- Find out as much as you can about the history of the property. Was it on the market before with another agent? Has a previous sale fallen through? Has the asking price changed? If the sellers have had trouble selling the property, they are more likely to accept a lower offer. Is the house already tenanted? Is it empty? Requiring full refurbishment or just minor repairs?

Making an offer

Call the estate agent; make your offer, which should be well below the asking price initially, or below market value (BMV) by 20% to 25% [cheeky!] of the asking price. Then be prepared to increase your offer, but set the maximum amount you can afford and stick to it. Remember: the figures need to stack up.

You may get a number of No's along the way. That's to be expected.

Ensure that the estate agent understands that you are a serious buyer, that you can move very quickly on the deal and that you have supporting documents to prove your financial position. They will usually ask for proof of funds for the deposit so make sure you have the necessary AIP that you can give or email to them.

The estate agent will then pass on your offer to the vendor

If you are successful, you will get the good news that your offer has been accepted. CONGRATULATIONS!

If you don't, don't despair. That's not the only great property opportunity.

Even so, sometimes, even after a house has been offered to someone else, until they have completed the deal, there's a possibility the sale may not go through. If so, the property might be put back in the market again.

This happened with one of the houses I offered to purchase. My offer was rejected.

Then, several months later, I found the same property advertised for sale again. This time, I put in an offer much lower than my original one – and it was accepted!

This is not a typical experience, so don't count on that happening.

That said, you can always move on to other properties if this one does not go through.

Once an offer is accepted, the estate agent will usually ask for the name of your solicitor or conveyancer so they can inform the seller and their solicitor. Your solicitor then can start the legal searches and process.

Mortgage Stuff

Your broker will proceed with the full mortgage application when you tell him your offer has been accepted. The lender (bank or building society) will then be informed and a surveyor will be appointed to visit the property and provide a mortgage valuation to confirm that the property provides sufficient security to offset the loan.

You normally have to pay a fee for this service, but some mortgage companies might waive the fee in order to win your business.

The lender will then advise if the mortgage can be granted, so you can address the financial requirements you agreed to in the offer.

Legal Stuff

Whist the financial process is going on, inform your conveyancer / solicitor that your offer has been accepted so s/he can proceed with the local searches etc.

If this is the first time you have used that solicitor/conveyancer, they will ask for proof of your identity; a copy of your passport plus proof of address, usually a utility bill or bank statement that will need to be certified by a professional person, such as a doctor, lawyer or school teacher.

Note: Lawyers and doctors will charge a fee for this service, so it is well worth shopping around. Near where I live, for instance, three legal firms quoted £5, £10, and £15 respectively to certify a copy of such a document.

Sometimes, the office of your solicitor/conveyancer may not be local to you so you will need to submit your identity evidence by post.

Once your identity is verified, your appointed conveyancer will then:-

1. draw up a draft contract or terms of engagement with you, setting out their charges and deposits
2. write to your seller's solicitor to confirm they are instructed and request a copy of the draft contract and any other details, such as the property's title and the standard forms detailing items included in the sale
3. examine the draft contract and supporting documents and raise enquiries with the seller's solicitor. You will be expected to go through the forms the seller has completed and let your solicitor know if you have any queries or concerns.

In particular you will want to double check the tenure of your new home: is it leasehold or freehold? I personally only deal with freehold property. If it is leasehold, don't rely on your solicitor to check the length of the lease. Leases below 80 years are a problem, can be costly to extend and you need to have owned the property for two years before you are eligible to do so. Leases under 60 years are best avoided.

4. do a set of searches such as:

- Local authority searches: are there development plans in your surrounding area? How about radon gas? This costs between £70 and £400 depending on the Local Authority and usually takes 1-2 weeks, but can take up to 6 weeks
- Check the 'title register' and 'title plan' at the Land Registry – these are the legal documents proving the seller's ownership.
- Check the flood risk – this is also done at the Land Registry
- Water authority searches – find out how you get your water and if any public drains on the property might affect extensions or building works.

- Location specific searches – examples of such searches include: Tin searches, Mining searches, Radon gas search, Environmental search from the Environmental Agency – which shows whether, for example, the plot used to be a landfill site

Survey

You would be well-advised to have your own survey done in order to obtain all the information you'll need about the structure and condition of your property. The valuation survey commissioned by your mortgage lender is merely to satisfy them that the property could be sold at auction to recover the amount of your debt should you default on the repayments.

There are a number of different types of surveys you could arrange, depending on the age of the house and how much you are prepared to spend.

For example:-

1. **Condition Survey Report** – this is a basic survey usually designed to complement a mortgage valuation, and provides a summary of risks to the building. This is rarely useful, and does not include any advice or valuation.

2. **Home Buyer's Report** – is a more detailed survey which tells you any obvious problems such as wet or dry rot, rising damp or subsidence. The surveyor will not look under floor coverings such as carpets – or even move junk mail that has accumulated while the property was empty to look at the floor (I speak from experience!) – or behind furniture, lift floor boards or inspect the roof, other than by looking at it from ground level. So any report they draw up is very limited. It includes a valuation and

insurance reinstatement value, but is usually full of caveats and exclusion clauses designed to protect the surveyor from negligence claims. For your purposes, it's almost worthless.

3. **Full Building Survey** – this is an expensive yet often a worthwhile investment as the report is extensive and detailed, and is usually appropriate for older, unusual or listed properties. It's also good to have a full building survey done if you intend to do some serious building refurbishment works. The surveyor will check behind walls, look between floors, above ceilings and inspect the attic or roof void. The report will include advice on repairs, estimated timings and costs, and advise you of potential damage to the property if you do not do the repairs. If specified, it can include insurance reinstatement costs and a market valuation. Such a survey can often be used to negotiate a further reduction in price before exchange of contracts – or may suggest you would be better off to cut your losses and withdraw from the purchase rather than buy a 'money pit'.

Building Insurance

Before exchange of contracts can take place your lender will require you to obtain Buildings Insurance for your new property. You are responsible for the property as soon as contracts have been exchanged, so it is in your interest to do so. If you are a member of an organisation such as the National Landlord Association (NLA), you can usually find service providers where you can get competitive and comprehensive insurance policy solutions.

Safety Regulations

In the UK, landlords must comply with a number of strict safety regulations designed to protect the tenants from avoidable hazards:-

1. Gas – there is a legal requirement that all gas appliances are checked and certified by a Gas Safe Registered engineer (Gas Safety Installation and Use Regulations 1988). The Gas Certificate record must be up to date and kept, and a copy given to your managing agent (if applicable) and to your tenant.

2. Electricity – the landlord has a legal duty to ensure all electrical appliances are safe. Landlords are legally liable if their tenants suffer injury or are put at risk because of faulty electrical goods or wiring, so it's recommended that you obtain an Electrical Equipment Safety Certificate (EESC). Although not a legal requirement, it is also advisable to have a Portable Appliance Test (PAT) if you are providing portable appliances – such as kettles, toasters and microwaves – in your rental property.

3. Furniture and Fittings – The Furniture and Furnishings (Fire Safety) Regulations 1993 makes it a criminal offence to let a property with upholstered items that do not comply with the safety regulations. The regulations apply to beds, mattresses, sofas, cushions and other soft furniture. These must all carry a label showing fire resistance. Any non-compliant furniture must be removed from your property before letting.

Signing Contracts

You will receive a draft contract from your conveyancer/solicitor who will have been in correspondence with you about what is covered, and ensure that all enquiries have been returned and are satisfactory, all the fixtures and fittings included in the purchase are what you expected, and a completion date has been agreed between the two parties, (usually between 4 – 12 weeks – but in the case of my current home it was only one week!)

Contracts need to be witnessed and signed. You will also need to provide a confirmation that you have made arrangements to transfer the deposit to your solicitor's account and that the funds will have cleared in time for exchange.

Visit the property again with the estate agent and check the fixtures and fittings listed in the contract to confirm that everything you paid for is still there and the house has not been damaged in any way.

Exchanging Contracts

Inform your solicitor when you want to exchange and complete. Your solicitor will then agree to this with the other party. Your solicitor will exchange contracts for you, and immediately inform you by phone, then confirm by post or email, or both, that you have exchanged.

If there is a chain in the purchase, the exchange could take longer. For example, A is buying B's property. B is buying C's property and C is buying D's property. If any of these sales do not complete, the exchange and sale completion could take longer or the purchase may not go ahead at all.

Once you have exchanged contracts, you are in a legally binding contract to buy the property. The seller can no longer accept another offer so you don't need to worry about being gazumped. Your solicitor will send you a statement showing the final figure to pay (which can sometimes include their professional fees and expenses) which will need to be cleared and in your solicitor's bank account at least one day before completion. If, however, you do not complete the purchase after exchange of contracts, you will lose your deposit and owe the seller more if the deposit was less than 10%.

Completion

This is normally set around mid-day on the specified date or when the seller's solicitor confirms that they have received all the money that is due. Once this happens, you will be informed that the keys to your new house will be ready for your collection and you can then move in or start the refurbishment works necessary. Hooray!

Thereafter

Your solicitor will tie up some loose ends, by paying the stamp duty land tax (if applicable). You will receive your legal documents about 20 days after completion, once your solicitor has sent them to the Land Registry, sent a copy of the title deeds to your mortgage lender who will hold them until you pay off your loan, and given you the bill for their payment, unless this has already been included previously.

Do ensure you gather all the paperwork from your purchase of the property, including estate agents' brochures, any notes, correspondence and copies of emails, to file away and keep safe for future reference.

Also remember to take pictures of the property before and after refurbishment and to keep in your file all correspondence, contracts, receipts etc.

Finding Tenants

Everybody wants the best tenant, the professional or family with high income, stable roots, excellent credit, solid references and a commitment to stay in the property forever, accepting regular rent increases and always paying on time....
For some that's a dream. For many, tenants cause nightmares!

So where do you find the best tenants?

From other great tenants, from organizations you respect, from schools and hospitals in the neighbourhood and from references.

You may find yourself placing adverts in the local paper, or online, and in all instances, make sure you get and check references – more than once!

Even if the money looks great, the potential seems solid and the track record appears positive, trust your gut. There's something to be said for walking away if you aren't feeling confident. Once a bad tenant is in, it's really tough to get them out!

What about Rent?

How much rent can you collect for your property? How soon will you be able to increase the rental income? What does the rent cover? Mortgage? Utilities (e.g. gas and electrics)? Is there parking? Do you permit tenants to keep pets in the property?
Check the average rental price of similar properties on property

portal websites such as Rightmove, Zoopla, Gumtree, FindAProperty, your local letting agent's websites or your local newspaper. Make sure you check how much other landlords are charging for similar houses, i.e. location, size of the house, number of rooms, whether the house is furnished or unfurnished, and the overall condition of the property. You will then have a realistic estimate of the current rate of rent that should be expected.

How will you collect your rent? Direct deposit? Pre-written cheques? Bank transfers? Or get a letting agent to do all the management on your behalf so you can sit back and wait for the money to go in your bank account month after month?

Make sure you understand how the legislation works in your marketplace around late payment of rent. Processes must be legally followed because they are usually slanted in favour of tenants – and you don't want to get "caught" in a legal "back-and-forth" battle.

A happy tenant = a happy landlord!

Tenancy Deposit Protection

If you rent your property on an AST (assured shorthold tenancy), if you self-manage your property portfolio, you must put your tenant's deposit in a government-backed tenancy deposit scheme (TDP). By law, a landlord or agent who receives a deposit for such a tenancy must protect the deposit. This must be done within 30 days of receiving the tenant's deposit. If you're appointing a letting agent to fully manage your property, they will arrange this for you – but do check yourself that they have done so! To learn more about tenancy deposit protection, go to https://www.gov.uk/tenancy-deposit-protection/overview

or https://www.tds.gb.com. If, on the other hand, you have appointed a letting agent to do the full management for you, protecting tenant's deposit is part of the service that they provide.

Chapter 10
Freedom: How I Did It

After the first year, I owned 1 student HMO and 3 houses let to families and professionals - and generated positive cash flow. I covered my income from my day j.o.b. and could confidently say goodbye to employee status and hello to being in the driver's seat.

Am I wealthy? Far from it.

Am I excited? Absolutely.

What do I wish I had known when I first started? In some ways, I'm glad I started where I did. I was determined, open, ready and hungry to learn and apply. I was on a mission. And with that, I was proactive and productive, serious and committed. I just wish I'd started earlier. Remember that push up reference? You have to go there to get here.

Does it stack up?

My "impossible dream" was to cover my salary with rental revenues – as quickly as possible. My timeline was ambitious: **1 year!**

How I managed to get into gear and stay on track was a function of the people I worked with, the information I collected, my research, my focus, dedication and willingness to do "whatever it takes", even if it was unpleasant, inconvenient, exhausting, scary and even dirty!

The objective: Passive Income for independence.

That is the beacon that helps me choose one property over another, to dig deeper than deep to get to the real story behind the property and the neighbourhood.

There have been times when I've had to be extra creative about locating funds. You might have to do that too. You'll be surprised what you can obtain when you apply your mind to locating leverage:

For example, I have an extra room in my home. When I have a new bill to pay or additional expenses coming up, like insurance, I contact the local language school and let them know I have space for a student, a temporary lodger for the duration of their course. They are most welcoming and always give me a student who stays for a short period such as 3 weeks, or up to 12 weeks at a time. I don't tend to have somebody long-term as I want to keep within the maximum allowable 'rent a room' relief of £4,250 per annum so I don't have to pay tax on the income; this has now been recently increased to £7,500 (for the tax year 2016/17), meaning I can have longer stays in future if I so wish.

Another resource is parking. I have three spaces in an area where there is a high demand for parking. I'm able to let that space and get additional income that way.

If your house is at the end of a terrace or a row, you might be able to rent advertising space on the side of your wall. (Of course, first make sure to check with your local council requirements for doing so as there might be restrictions in your area.)

What resources do you have that other people may want or need? How can you provide help and assistance in exchange for financial consideration?

It's there. You just have to focus on it.

LOOKING AHEAD:

Now that I'm out of that hamster wheel and have my monthly "nut" covered financially, I have more choices going forward.

With my system in place, I can replicate what I've done and double the number of houses I acquired in the first round.

I can refinance what I have in place as it increases in value, all the while offsetting my mortgages and receiving positive cash flows from every house I own.

Now I'm free and have more precious TIME; time to spend with the family, time to learn more about new strategies in property acquisition, time to look for other opportunities for wealth creation.

My path is clear. I can choose how I want to devote my time and energy going forward. Choice is the ultimate Freedom.

If you've read this book from cover to cover, well done. I hope the reading gave you ideas, incentive, insights and inspiration to Choose ACTION to reach your financial goals.

If there's one idea I hope you got from this experience, it's that it's never too late. Armed with the right frame of mind, the right resources, the determination to keep on keeping on, you can turn your WHY? into a WHY NOT?!

Visit my website: www.landlordaccelerated.com to remain in the loop, to share your experiences, and to find out more about "what's next".

Summary

Mary Bautista-Harman is a former IT professional who came from difficult beginnings to build financial independence, literally from the ground up.

Immigrating to the UK from her native Philippines, Mary was determined to create a life of freedom from financial worry and anxiety.

Although Mary was well into mature adulthood when she took her first step, she made the move with intention, with focus and with a burning desire to beat the odds on her own - in record-breaking time!

Not a manual or workbook, this writing documents a woman on a mission. It's loaded with actual case studies of Mary's "life in the property acquisition trenches", with details of how she achieved it – and how you can too.

"Landlord Accelerated, How to create residual income that replaces your current salary in LESS THAN A YEAR!" is about commitment, dedication, and down-to-earth human motivation. A combination "how to" and "how I did", this first book by an inspired and inspiring woman points the way for anyone who wants to fast-track through property acquisition to achieve financial freedom – at any age!

Testimonials

"Mary is very committed to making a success of her property career. During her three days of mentorship, she carefully planned her strategy, then followed the path she set for herself. Once focused on her goal, with careful planning, followed by lots of action, Mary reached her financial freedom figure in a very timely fashion. It was a joy to work with Mary." Shirley Harwood, Mentor, Property Investor, Landlord

"In this book Mary has given a great understanding of what is needed to succeed in property investing with a combination of clear and simple advice and case studies of what she actually did to achieve her target of replacing her income with property within a year. This book is a practical guide, giving both the positive and potential issues, which I would recommend to anyone thinking of starting their own venture into property investing." Peter Lawrence, Host of Sutton Property Investors Network (pin) Meeting

"This isn't one of those vague, aspirational self-help books. It's a hard-headed, comprehensive and tightly written by an author who really knows the territory." A.G, Wimbledon Landlord

"A great read, you will gain a clear insight into Mary's journey along her path to becoming a professional property Investor. Mary is a shining example of how education, focus, determination and of course most importantly ACTION will always create success." Debra Rice, Presenter, Trainer, Mentor, Fielding Financial

"Readers will be familiar with the acronym 'kiss' – keep it short and simple – which the author has certainly adopted in the writing of this book. She has applied the same principle in her approach to property investment by following a simple strategy that has produced results in a short time." Barbara Frank, BFrankCommunication!

"When I started investing in property, I was fortunate to have personal advice from the author. I cannot recommend her book too highly." Paul Pry, magazine article author

"This book illuminates corners of the world of property investment. It provides a valuable and often an entertaining guide for the novice investor in property." Olwen Wright, teacher of elocution, professional actress

"People interested in investing in property for the first time will find this to be just the book they need. " G E Commander, retired business owner and property investor

"A concise, readable and informative book that every aspiring property investor should keep close to hand for ready reference." Julie Formoso, UK and oversees property investor

Reference Web Sites:

National Landlord Association
www.landlords.org.uk

Landlords National Property Group
http://www.lnpg.co.uk/

HMRC – Her Majesty's Revenue and Customs
https://www.gov.uk/government/organisations/hm-revenue-customs

Right move
www.rightmove.co.uk

Zoopla
www.zoopla.co.uk/

Prime location
www.primelocation.com

nethouseprices
www.nethouseprices.com

Dash
www.dashservices.org.uk

To learn more about tenancy deposit protection, go to https://www.gov.uk/tenancy-deposit-protection/overview or https://www.tds.gb.com.

Landlord Accreditation Wales
www.welshlandlords.org.uk
Land Registry House Price Search
http://houseprices.landregistry.gov.uk/